TIME TO TEACH
TIME TO REACH

Expert teachers give voice to the power of
RELATIONAL TEACHING

Nat Damon

Foreword by Dr. Rob Loe

Acknowledgements

Time to Teach: Time to Reach is dedicated to the teaching colleagues and mentors who guided me through my formative years in teaching and in school leadership. Bob Hurlbut, Ed Foley, Connie Chapin, Lloyd Griffith, Linda Knight, Catherine Stock, Liz Resnick, Tom Hudnut, Ray Michaud, Reveta Bowers. I am grateful for the many who have helped shape the final edition of *Time to Teach: Time to Reach*, most especially Janice Pieroni, Gill Wing, and Tara Rehl. Thanks to Ric Torres for his love and support for this project.

Thanks also to Dr. Robert Loe and Relational Schools Foundation for their support in building a partnership focused on applying the research contained in these pages.

This book is also dedicated to current and future teachers and parents. We are all responsible for cultivating a fertile learning environment in our homes and communities. Teaching is heart-work and great teaching appears when the student is ready.

Therefore my final dedication is to my sister Lin Damon, who prepared me to learn from the lessons that exist all around us.

Address: Relational Schools
Future Business Centre
King's Hedges Road
Cambridge
CB4 2HY
United Kingdom

Email: office@relationalschools.org

Website: relationalschools.org

© 2018

Nat Damon has asserted his right under the Copyright, Designs and Patents Act, 1988, to be identified as Author of this work.

First published 2018

Printed in USA

Photo credits

P18 Chris Gonyaw
P23 John Gillooly
P26 Juliet Youssef
P31 Vito Cheong
P49 Kate LaPine
P57 Nat Damon
P60 Ville Multanen
P73 Lakeside School
P80 MacKenzie Hennessey
P82 The Episcopal School of Los Angeles
P98 Davey Huang
P102 Amber Ford
P115 Salvador Rodarte
P127 Vayda
P132 Nori Curtis
P136 Matthew Arnold
P151 Jennifer Godwin-Minto
P162 Oscar Gomez
P175 Hunter Barnhardt
Backcover: Mark Grey, Samuel Verbi

Design and layout: Mark Knight

Printed by Edition One

Cover photo: Chris Gonyaw

Contents

Foreword

Time is the currency of relationships

The political scientist, Robert D. Putnam, observed in 2000, that *"Americans are so hard working they no longer have free time in which to see each other. The amount of time friends spend at each other's houses has dropped 35% since the 1970s while, at home, families are a third less likely to eat together. There is also far less participation in civic affairs: over the past 30 years the time Americans devote to supporting a political party has halved...in terms of social capital [he argued], America has become truly impoverished."*[1]. The contention is that the U.S., and other Western societies, have become time poor and time poverty has led to relational bankruptcy. We're too busy now; too busy for each other.

Brooks Hatlen, Stephen King's fictional character, imprisoned in Shawshank for nearly 50 years (1905–1954) reflects on the world as it is now, in a letter to his friends, who are still imprisoned. Disorientated by a new pace to life, he cannot reconcile his experiences. The world, he laments, *"went and got itself in a big damn hurry"*. That was his perception then. But it's ours too.

Surveys reveal heightened perceptions of being busy. The American Psychology Association have published the "Stress in America™" survey annually since 2007, which measures attitudes and perceptions of stress among the general public and identifies leading sources of stress, common behaviors used to manage stress, and the impact of stress on our lives. It is believed that over half of the 550 million working days lost annually in the U.S. from absenteeism are stress-related and that one in five of all last-minute no-shows are due to job stress.[2]

---

1   Putnam, R. (2000), This Week, 9th December 2000, p.12
2   The European Agency for Safety and Health at Work (reported: https://www.stress.org/workplace-stress/)

That said, when you consider this empirically, we are not necessarily "busier" than we have been. If you take a longer-term view, statutory working hours have changed relatively little in the last 30 years. If you go back to the 19th century, the average working week for a man or woman was, on average, 60 hours. Now it's 34 hours (OECD, 2017). Clearly, whilst the working day of many will have remained consistent in length for many years (indeed, the narrative for some will be steadily increasing hours) there is evidence that the average length of the working week has actually declined, but if you interview people, irrespective, they will say they are busier.

I think this is true of a teacher's experience as well. It certainly was mine. In the UK context, the beginning of my career coincided with a government-commissioned review into workload by PricewaterhouseCoopers (PwC). Teachers were benchmarked against other occupations and it was found that *"teachers and headteachers work[ed] more intensive weeks than other comparable managers and professionals."*[3] The report, referred to the School Teachers' Review Body (2002), calculated that the average teacher in the United Kingdom, in 2002, was working around 52 hours a week in term time. Given the current recruitment and retention crisis, you would think that teachers are working significantly longer hours now, than they were then. And yet, when the Department for Education published the 2016 Teachers' Working Time Survey in February last year, it showed that teachers were working on average 54.4 hours per week. The picture is no different in the U.S. A recent report from the Bill & Melinda Gates Foundation (2012),[4] estimates the average American teacher's working week to be around 53 hours. It is a relatively consistent picture.

And yet perception is so often reality. Teachers *feel* under greater strain because the way we all experience time varies.

An hour worked now, it is thought, is twenty-five times more productive than an hour worked in 1830. This is largely due to the impact of new technologies. And it is those same technologies, like social media, that have simultaneously changed our perceptions of time. With the acceleration of news production, leaders are expected to respond in minutes or hours, rather than the more leisurely pace of British Victorian political cycles where people might take days or weeks to comment.

Social media has had an even more profound impact on our social interactions. Whereas time was once rigidly zoned, we now "share" time

---

3   School Teachers' Review Body (2002). "Special Review of Approaches to Reducing Teacher Workload". London: The Stationery Office.
4   Gates Foundation (2012) Primary Sources: America's Teachers on the Teaching Profession (http://www.scholastic.com/primarysources/download.asp)

with many different people. Part of the way technology gets used (the way we employ it) is to control, or attempt to govern, the dimensions of human existence; mechanically coordinate the very dimensions of space. We can now be everywhere simultaneously. If we are connected through a social media app, such as Twitter or Facebook, we can be in each other's lives all the time. Our devices are now always on us, and always on.

The Enlightenment encouraged us to think about time in different ways. It's almost impossible to get our heads around this but in the ancient world, argued EP Thompson[5], there was a much greater sense of time being cyclical. The passing of the seasons, the marking of the festivals; they would always come back around. Looking at the work of the anthropologist, Evans Pritchard, in his book *The Nuer: A description of Modes of Livelihood and Political Institutions of a Nilotic People* (1940), he found a people without a word for time and a very different concept of it. Their timepiece was, in effect, the cattle, with each day structured according to the rhythms of the animals, which allowed time to be perceived in terms of relationships to routines, commonly shared and experienced.

Pre-industrialization, the lack of standardized timekeeping meant that an individual's own timepiece created mini time zones. It is only with the advent of the railways that standardization becomes mandated: the time at one end of the line needs to be consistent with the time at the other end. That ushered in standardized factory systems of production and mechanistic approaches to human resource management. With the steam engine starting at 6am in the morning, everyone could now be expected to clock-on at that same time and with the productivity and accountability for that time now measured in scruples.

Arguably the greatest invention of the industrial revolution was the clock. With it came a rejection of approximation. We went from, "I'll see you in the morning" to "I'll see you at 11:45pm". From, "no worries, I was delayed as well, and besides, we've got the whole afternoon" to "apologies, I've got another person coming to see me in 35 minutes; let's keep this short and to the purpose." We begin to hear phases like, "I can only give you an hour of my time, I'm afraid." People are able to watch the time on their wrists. Distraction technologies discreetly intrude when you are running over time; when another appointment is imminent or another person is anxious to get hold of you. Alexander Graham Bell would never have imagined you could dispense with the ringing of a telephone when your watch could vibrate and warn you that others need your attention. And we are always checking them. It is no different to the developing ways in which we actively monitor steps

5   Thompson, E.P. (1967) *Past & Present* No. 38, pp. 56-97

or calories. Once you're told to watch calories, food is just not the same any more.

Once people could accurately measure time, and chunk it up into smaller and smaller divisions, it changed our perception of it, forever.

With this change came great pressures, amplified by religious thought-leadership of the time. One can feel the impact of the protestant work ethic in the late 18th and 19th centuries by exploring writing of the period. The Methodist John Wesley, who himself rose at 4am each morning, wrote a sermon called "The Duty and Advantage of Early Rising" (1809), in which he claimed that lying in bed was physically unhealthy. He warns, poetically, against, *"soaking so long between warm sheets, the flesh is, as it were parboiled...becomes soft and flabby. The nerves in the meantime are quite unstrung."*[6] In 1830, Hannah More published the following lines in *Early Rising*, once again warning against the evil of being still:

Thou silent murderer, Sloth, no more
My mind imprison'd keep;
Nor let me waste another hour
With thee, thou felon, Sleep.[7]

Like More, Wesley entreated his listeners to redeem every passing moment. Time becomes more scarce, more valuable and in that context leisure becomes suspect.

You would hope that labor-saving devices and the enormous resources dedicated to the leisure industry should mean that life at least feels more gentle. In 1880 men had very little leisure time: only about 1.8 hours per day over the course of a year. Fogel (2000) estimates that the amount of leisure time we enjoy has more than tripled in the 21st century. And yet we are far less likely to be at leisure – not for want of opportunity. *"Free* time" is costly, and a rarity. In thinking like this, we've commoditized time and, as Pete Nicolas[8] persuasively argues, it is something we can now trade in and its value can rise and fall.

The defining characteristics of a commodity are twofold: firstly, it needs to be limited. You can only trade something if not everybody has access to it. It is why we don't trade in seawater because of its abundance; you can't sell it. But if something is limited you can trade it. Secondly, it has to be open to private ownership. You can only trade something if there can be individual

6   Wesley, J. (1809), "The Duty and Advantage of Early Rising: a sermon on Ephesians 5: v16", John Jones
7   More, H. (1846), *The Works of Hannah More*, Harper and Brothers
8   Brooks, E. and Nicolas P. (2015) *Virtually Human: Flourishing in a digital world.* Inter-Varsity Press

owners' rights. One only has to explore common idiomatic phrases related to time, so often taken for granted they have become overfamiliar, to understand our attitudes toward it. We are often asked how we "spend our time"; told that we are "running out of time"; assured that time can be "borrowed" ("time *is – literally* – money"); we apologize that we have taken up so much of someone's time and hear the humble assurance in return: "not at all – it's my time, not your time". We can trade it backwards and forwards.

Values like productivity, efficiency or speed are always calculated using time as the key variable. Every second counts, *"every minute must be maximized. Since we cannot stop the escaping moments, we have our machines give us the next best thing: two moments crammed into one...we need miss nothing. In fact, we can't. In 'real time' we live in two minds, three tenses and four continents all at once and buy back the bits lost in transition. We have become so good at mastering time, nanoseconds weigh heavy on our minds."* (Powers, 2004)[9]

Work and life become imbalanced, not because quantified working time has formally increased but because working practices have bled into the fabric of our leisure time. We take urgent calls in the car rather than making more trivial conversation with the passengers. Recreation time with our family and friends in front of the television becomes a tertiary activity because we can respond to a few emails whilst pretending to be present and participatory. Putnam was wrong. This is not a paucity of time; this is a perversion, a corruption, of the time we have. We have degraded it, or to continue the metaphor, truly devalued it. Like a currency, its stock has fallen dramatically because we have assumed time is endless, ubiquitous, growing in abundance as we become more efficient. True time poverty, (defined by insufficient quantity and inadequate quality of time), has led to relational bankruptcy.

This is a massive problem because we know that relational wealth, not material wealth, is a stronger indicator of happiness throughout our lives. The Harvard Study of Adult Development, a longitudinal study that follows men over 75 years to identify the psychosocial predictors of healthy aging, found that the quality of our relationships at age 50 is a far better predictor of physical health than cholesterol levels. That it is our relationships, and the quality/quantity of time that we invest in them, that enable us to be psychologically more resilient, disrupt mental and physical decline, and are much better predictors of human flourishing than social class, IQ, or even our genetic makeup.

By contrast, several studies have demonstrated the effects (both on individual

9   Powers, R. (2004), "Introduction", *The Paris Review Book for Planes, Trains and Waiting Rooms*, New York: Picador

educational attainment as well as on society) of broken relationships: defined here as "non-intact families" (Roberts et al. 2009), "fractured" or "non-stable" home environments (CSJ, 2013) or "insecure attachments", which can be in the home, with teachers or amongst a child's peer group (Marsh, 2007). Where relationships, as described above, are dysfunctional, the negative impact on student outcomes is significant. Young people are at higher risk of mental illness, at risk of manifesting aggressive or withdrawn behaviors, and of being more likely to underachieve academically and experience persistent and longitudinal social exclusion. And yet, we know that where attachment in the classroom context is more secure, relationships can surmount social inequality; where they are weak or fragile, however, evidence suggests they reinforce educational disadvantage.

And relationships, reaching out to people in a way that forms deep connection, take time. You can't create relationships instantly any more than you can instantly mature a tree or its fruit. In the end, whilst we might tell ourselves that "quality time" is more important, there is no substitute for quantity time. You need it to build relationships; you need it to maintain relationships.

That is why Nat Damon's book is so valuable and so timely.

Time itself has been the currency that has fed and sustained the book. It emanates from deep reflection; the physical and mental distance of the writer. It is based on teachers who have been in the profession "a long time" and with it comes more than knowledge of the profession but great wisdom. Lastly, and more fundamentally, it both campaigns for, and shapes best practice of, time itself. There is simultaneously an advocating voice in the text ("it's high time we...") which calls for different priorities in education, as well as a practical voice ("make time for..." i.e. prioritize, foreground, see as important) which provides a pedagogical framework to encourage the most valuable classroom practices to come to the surface.

As Damon himself argues, this is the stuff of genuine teaching and learning. Teaching that foregrounds time as its most essential element: "This is the relational teaching that arises when we have time to teach and time to reach."

Time to go...

Dr. Robert Loe
Relational Schools Foundation, February 2018

Prelude: time for the obvious

At first glance, the theme of this book might seem quite obvious. We all know that teaching requires the development of relational skills: building connection, establishing trust, acquiring authenticity, prioritizing reflection, cultivating hope and encouraging exploration. If as a teacher I picked up this book and thumbed through it, I would rightfully question its added value. Two hundred pages about six elements of teaching that I already know. We all already know. If it seems so obvious, would it be a worthwhile read?

But let's reframe this for a moment. Let's look at this book not as spotlighting the obvious, but instead the *essential*. Let's read into its pages and open our eyes to the voices of expert teachers who speak from the raw depths of qualitative experience. As we delve further into this book, let's align our deepest-rooted beliefs about great teaching within the context of today's data and metrics-based society. Let's read into these pages the voices that give honor to the relational and human elements of teaching. Let's recall the picture of a curious five-year-old on his first day of kindergarten. Our social media feeds are full of them in August and September: "Look at Johnny making his way to his first day of 'real' school!" Now think about what must be going on in Johnny's head and heart. *I am new to this. I don't know what to expect. I am away from my parents. I do not know my surroundings. I don't know anyone…*

Let's look now at Johnny's teacher and the thoughts that he must have going through his mind. *How will I connect with Johnny? How will I gain his trust in me so he feels safe and sound? How much of "me" will I share with him in order to open him up to my position as authority figure and human being? How will I motivate Johnny to explore without fear of being wrong? How will I create enough time for Johnny to reflect on what he learned? How will I maintain hope in Johnny (and cultivate Johnny's hope in himself) when January hits and the fun of school becomes overwhelmed by frustration?*

Lastly, let's look at the outside world Johnny is growing up in. A world with newspaper headlines like this one from the *Financial Times* that reads, "Should Androids Really Shape Children's Minds?"[1] As the digital age enmeshes itself more deeply into the world of education and child development, what will it *"educere"* (i.e. "lead out") from our children? Will it be rote facts? Will it be critical thinking? Will it encourage collaboration and creativity or will it be all about splitting hairs on the student scorecard? Most importantly, what role will technology have in Johnny's education vis-à-vis his teacher's? If a robot can never truly replace a human being because it literally has no soul, what might get lost as technology bites away at more and more minutes of Johnny's school year? Are we destined to create a future of automatons? Schools are already being compared to factories; will they now spit out assembly line robots instead of assembly line workers?

The micro-moments also count.

Time to Teach: Time to Reach focuses on the relational elements expert teachers bring into their classrooms. These elements (Trust, Exploration, Authenticity, Connection, Hope, Reflection: TEACH-R) are the same used by Confucius and Aristotle, by Booker T. Washington and Anne Sullivan. They are the human elements that every child can intuitively relate to. These elements are imprinted as children watch their teachers with wide eyes, active skepticism, and hunger for comfort. This is why it is not enough to plan effective lessons and master the content. The micro-moments also count. Students are looking at how their teachers manage their day-to-day interactions: with each other, with students, parents, administration, support staff, the groundskeeper. They are retaining lessons from these micro-moments. The accumulation of these micro-moments will shape the way they interact with their adult world.

The teaching life sustains itself through *connection*, which takes time to build. *Trust* is an essential glue in the school community, and it takes a nanosecond to break. *Hope* gives teachers the energy to scale the steepest challenges, and it requires time to cultivate. We seek *authenticity* in ourselves and others, and *reflection* time is key toward this happening. The joy of *exploration* through shared inquiry requires time so that the "Eureka Moment" can result from the steadfast efforts toward proving a hypothesis. All of these examples stem from the acronym TEACH-R.

Every voice in this book is from an expert teacher. The reasoning behind this is simple: only by interviewing expert teachers can the relational elements of teaching be discussed. These expert teachers know their subject up, down, and all-around. They could teach their lessons at a moment's notice because they already have done so tens of dozens of times in the past. They can push

---

1   https://www.ft.com/content/f3cbfada-668e-11e7-8526-7b38dcaef614

the "what" of content matter aside and instead focus on the "how" of its delivery.

This is an important point to underscore: in order to best discuss the elements of relational teaching, one must be confident enough in his or her subject matter in order to be able to put it aside and articulate the nuances that go into expert instructional delivery. Transcending all the examples of relational teaching in *Time to Teach: Time to Reach* is the belief that content mastery comes first and foremost. Otherwise, it's putting the cart before the horse. One simply cannot be an expert teacher without possessing deep knowledge of their subject area. In this book's interviewees, expert content knowledge is a given.

The teachers interviewed are K–12 schoolteachers from independent, charter, and public schools in the U.S., UK and Finland. They teach in self-contained elementary school classrooms and departmentalized secondary school classrooms. We conducted the interviews face-to-face whenever possible, and through phone and Skype sessions. Each teacher was given focus questions to prepare for our interviews, and our conversations broadened organically from there.

Time to Teach: Time to Reach spotlights the voices of teachers so that readers can learn directly from the experts. Every teacher in the following pages is not only expert at their craft, but also expert at articulating it. Everyone can benefit from such wisdom. Teachers new to the profession can find a roadmap for their future growth. Veteran teachers can identify with the perspectives being expressed. Parents can deepen their understanding of the teaching profession and approach teacher interactions with more empathy. By focusing on the relational elements of teaching, we are reminded of the essential need for time (an increasingly valued yet diminishing resource of today's modern world): the time to teach and the time to reach.

> Transcending all the examples of relational teaching in *Time to Teach: Time to Reach* is the belief that content mastery comes first and foremost.

Eric Wlasak

Introduction

"The task of education is not to teach subjects: it is to teach students."

Sir Ken Robinson, *Out of Our Minds: Learning to be Creative*

After over two decades working in the United States as a teacher and administrator, I found myself on sabbatical in London eager to write about teaching from a physical and mental distance. As educators know, the school year offers extremely limited time for reflection and restoration. Over the summer, there are academic years to close out, summer programs to run, workshops, seminars, and other teacher training in which to participate, and upcoming academic years to prepare. Only a sabbatical would provide me with the time required to meditate on teaching and my 25-year experience with this uniquely human profession.

However, during this period of reflection, I realized that my zeal for the humanistic and qualitative elements of teaching had become to a large extent overrun by a

My zeal for the humanistic and qualitative elements of teaching had become to a large extent overrun by a movement to define effective teaching through a quantitative lens.

movement to define effective teaching through a quantitative lens. Business-speak increasingly describes this human profession (student work as "data", assessment as "metrics", families as "stakeholders", schools being "driven by dashboards"). Standardized testing has become ubiquitous and quite often misused (for example, when it becomes the key indicator of teacher performance). Light-speed technological developments risk turning students into numbers and learning into a commodity. I had the foreboding sense that the qualitative heart of teaching was being replaced by the quantitative, and it concerned me deeply.

Yet I found hope while conducting research for this book. This is because every teacher I interviewed spoke about the timeless importance of relational teaching. They work in public, private, and charter schools in the United States, the United Kingdom, and Finland. And they all possess 10 or more years of classroom experience.

High quality teaching cannot be seen as a mechanical exercise.

Why 10 or more years? Researchers Vanessa Rodriguez and Michelle Fitzpatrick speak of how important it is to recognize the time it takes to become an expert teacher. They write about "how unlikely it is that adequate training to prepare for this process could take place in a five-week summer program. It is also unlikely that even after three years of teaching, a teacher will have mastered how to practice this complex cognitive task within the context of a classroom."[2]

In *Visible Learning and the Science of How We Learn*, co-authors John Hattie and Gregory Yates state, "Expert teachers…actively shape the classroom world and skillfully entice their students into becoming motivated learners sharing the same learning goals as the teacher. But to get to this point entails considerable knowledge and personal investment over 5 to 10 years of development." Much like Malcolm Gladwell's "10,000 Hour Rule", Hattie and Yates claim that becoming an expert teacher requires years of practice. They explain this by focusing on the relational elements of expert teaching. "High quality teaching cannot be seen as a mechanical exercise. Instead, it hinges on developing a relationship with a group of young human beings who have come to trust and respect the goals that their teacher has for them."[3] They regard teaching as a relational endeavor built on trust and mutual respect, both for the goals of the classroom and those within who strive together to achieve those goals.

---

2   Rodriguez, Vanessa (2014), *The Teaching Brain* (New York: The New Press), p.36
3   Hattie, John and Yates, Gregory (2014), *Visible Learning and the Science of How We Learn* (London: Routledge Press), p.109

By focusing on the relational aspects of teaching, we return to the essence of what defines a classroom. It is a space for learning, of course, yet in its optimal form, a classroom is also a space for individual and collective cognitive, emotional, social, and moral growth. In its healthiest state, a classroom accelerates the spectrum of growth in its students, and reinforces the values and expectations that result in positive outcomes. In an age in which children are barraged 24/7 by technology and media, the relational teacher recognizes that the classroom can serve as a haven from the storms outside.

We are experiencing a dynamic and disruptive period in the world of K–12 education. Schools are redefining themselves, using technology in meaningful ways, and incorporating flipped, blended, and personalized pedagogy. Schools are opening up their classrooms, eliminating walls as a way for students and teachers to physically bump against each other with their ideas. Many schools now have maker-spaces, where STEM work can be accomplished in an engineering-based "lab." Parents are kept informed at a level far deeper than before the days of push-pages. In terms of feedback, the online grade books available today can take data and crunch, assess, and synthesize it into the most eye-catching graphs imaginable. When we assign projects aimed at getting students to go deeply into research, the world is literally at their fingertips via search engines, databases, and online libraries.

None of this, however, changes the fact that without a human leading the classroom, true learning does not easily take place.

If you were to ask a teacher about whether there is a perfect way to learn, you would likely be told that learning cannot be perfectly engineered; that it is impossible to design a flawless curriculum, execute a perfect pedagogy, or implement precise feedback. This is because we are human beings working in a human profession. We have individual learning styles, traits, and personalities.

Without a human leading the classroom, true learning does not easily take place.

Acknowledging that learning is impossible to perfect is not a cop-out. Rather, it is a realization – an *understanding* – that teaching to a classroom of different learning styles, diverse mindsets, and developing personalities necessarily results in varied outcomes. Factor in the varying student emotions, the family environments from which students arrive each morning, the sense of support from parents, administrators, and colleagues, and the variables become clear: teaching is messy because people are messy.

In truth, this lack of predictability is exactly what fires most teachers up. It reinforces our sense of possibility: the gold nugget buried in a student's ambiguous response; the tenth attempt at a math problem that finally achieves the correct answer; or the clearly defended thesis that results from one-on-one meetings between teacher and student followed by the student spending days writing in isolation. None of these rewards can be quantitatively assessed. The pathways are interpersonal and deeply relational. Walking on these pathways is what draws people into teaching year after year.

This is why teachers rightfully see themselves as artists, counselors, spiritual leaders, content experts, and coaches. Students remember teachers for years after the last day of school because of these qualitative aspects. Robert ("Chip") Williams, a Middle school history teacher at Learning Works Charter School in Los Angeles, California, says, "I relate teaching to that song, 'Light My Lamp from Your Lamp'. When you light my lamp, your light doesn't diminish but only gets stronger from sharing it with me, and I want to share it with others. This is the transmission that comes in the classroom."

> Expert teachers design their teaching around the principle that learning is a social endeavor.

We spent our most formative years in the presence of teachers. We listened to their inflections, sighs, and silences using one ear to learn content and the other to learn character. We watched with wide eyes wired north to our brains and south to our hearts. How our teachers reacted, responded, commanded, endured, shared, stupefied, and inspired critically calibrated our moral compass.

One of my most memorable teachers was James ("Jim") Connolly, who was my Junior Year English teacher at Milton Academy in Milton, Massachusetts. Mr. Connolly opened my eyes to American literature in a way no other teacher had. He generated a classroom of mutual respect, which made me feel safe offering my opinions without fear of being shot down. His classroom became a haven for me. I respected Mr. Connolly because he knew his material inside out and upside-down, yet he didn't pander or proselytize. Rather, he explored and investigated and he brought me along on the journey. He challenged me unlike any English teacher had before, and I worked harder for him than anyone previous because I knew he knew me.

He was inspired by a teacher whose impact on him was strikingly identical to his impact on me. "I was not a perfect student growing up. Then I read *The Great Gatsby*. Tom and Daisy Buchanan dug into me. Literature wasn't something you took for the grade – you learned something more. It changed the way I started to read, and this realization came to me with the help of

Jim Connolly

my English professor at the time." Without his teacher's impact, my English teacher might not have been Mr. Connolly. I would not have benefitted from his relational way of teaching, and I would not have dipped back into the well of his wisdom over my quarter-century as an English teacher and administrator.

Mr. Connolly's influence on me will remain with me throughout my life. The impact he had on me – the lessons I observed through an entire year of his influence – lives on not just in me, but also in the students I taught as an English teacher. His listening skills, impartiality, excitement about literature, and ability to draw out the universal human qualities of lust, jealousy, insecurity, emptiness, and rage that Tom and Daisy Buchanan experience were passed on through my students as well. A career spent in the classroom is a career without finality. Rather, a teacher's legacy lives on in perpetuity, existing in the relational exchange between teacher and student – as from one lighted lamp to another.

Expert teachers design their teaching around the principle that learning is a social endeavor. As Jonnie Noakes, Head of Teaching and Learning at England's renowned Eton College said during our interview, "I think that the relationship between teacher and pupil is incredibly important to the learning that goes on in schools. And I'm talking not just about the learning of values of attitudes and dispositions that are picked up as part of the ethos of the classroom. I'm also talking about the academic learning that goes on. This is because in schools learning is a social activity. Therefore, those relationships are keenly important." We will focus on those teacher–student relationships as described through the voices of the expert teachers themselves.

While conducting these interviews, I noticed how many teachers were lamenting the lack of time. The message I kept receiving is that time has become a diminished resource. Technology, testing, communication, and professional development have all been added to the job description of a present-day educator. *Time to Teach: Time to Reach* gives real-world examples of what happens when teachers reclaim time to connect, explore, reflect, build trust, and channel and restore hope through relational teaching.

The spiritual life of children needs to be reinforced in the classroom. It's important for teachers to tap into it.

When this time is reclaimed, the spiritual side of teaching reveals itself. Reveta Bowers, the 40-year Head of School at The Center for Early Childhood Education in West Hollywood, California says it best. "The spiritual life of children needs to be reinforced in the classroom. It's important for teachers to tap into it – to teach to the spirit of the child. This is the opposite of layering on expectations to the child. Rather, it's venturing within so as to pull the creativity, wonder and imagination out. It's all about connecting with the inner world of the child in order to engage and teach." Relational teachers know that establishing a strong relationship comes first. Only afterwards can the teacher "ventur(e) within" and "pull the creativity, wonder and imagination out." The chapter, "Time to Explore" will provide a closer look at this process, which involves safety (to explore unbounded) and connection (from teacher to student).

Relational teaching is predicated on an established connection between teacher and student as well as student and student. Eric Wlasak, fourth grade teacher and Diversity and Equity Coordinator at The Village School in Los Angeles, California, honors the beneficiaries of relational teaching when he says, "I deal with the most important person in someone's life. Times 25." Or 35. Or 45. Given the range of class sizes in today's schools, it is no wonder teachers are a precious commodity. While the joys of teaching are obvious to any onlooker, a teacher knows that behind the glimmering eyes is a mind divided. Not only is there content to be shared, but there are differentiating ways to deliver it – individualized to the unique learning styles of each student in the classroom.

Those glimmering eyes are scanning, scoping, and sequencing which students are paying attention and which are not, and whether students are nodding to show understanding or to disguise confusion. They are processing the overall health of the classroom climate. All of this is going on simultaneously and actively; longitudinally and continuously; behind the glimmering eyes of the teacher as they nod, gesture, and command a student to deliver a response. "Samantha," Todd Whitten, a history teacher at Burlington High School in Burlington, Massachusetts, beckons, "You haven't contributed for a while, yet I can tell you've got something to share…"

Time to Teach: Time to Reach is the end product of a lengthy process of harmonically weaving expert teacher voices around the central question, "what do you really do?" This book follows in the model of Parker Palmer's seminal work, *The Courage to Teach*. The purpose is identical: to inspire teachers to use "courage" (the "heart-word", as celebrated by scholar and speaker Brené Brown) as they run their classrooms while spotlighting the relational elements they incorporate into their teaching.

> Is the end product of a lengthy process of harmonically weaving expert teacher voices around the central question, "what do you really do?"

These expert teachers bring their offerings of dreams and doubts; success and failures; ambitions and abandonments. Most importantly, they bring their "arête" – their *excellence of any kind* related to the calling and spiritual endeavor of the millennia-old art of teaching. By transferring their wisdom to present and future teachers, they help move the relational element of teaching to center stage, benefitting the next generations of learners and perhaps even the scope and shape of our society's future.

Jen Dohr

Time to connect

"Human beings are happier, more cooperative and productive, and more likely to make positive changes in their behavior when those in positions of authority do things *with* them, rather than *to* or *for* them."

Laura Mirsky and Steve Korr, International Institute for Restorative Practices[4]

"Only connect! Only connect the prose and the passion, and both will be exalted, and human love will be seen at its height. Live in fragments no longer."

E. M. Forster[5]

The relationship between teacher and student is based on learning expectations and predicated on connection. The more a teacher connects with students, the better the probability that students will learn. Yet connection is not achieved merely through being kind, engaging, or theatrical. While there is a place for acting in teaching, the deepest connections are formed through the exposure of vulnerabilities and honesty: the revelation of the true self. It is through being human that human connections develop.

4   DeMeo, Stephen (2016), *The End Before the Beginning* (Butte, MT: Educe Press), p.40
5   Forster, E. M. (1910/1989), *Howard's End* (New York, NY: Vintage Classics), p.195

Therefore, a relational teacher gauges how to balance being professional with being human. Students can smell insincerity with acuity; yet they also need to rely on the integrity and maturity of the adult teacher in the classroom. Teaching requires a constant awareness of this line, and expert teachers are able to walk it with lofty results. It is true that in my experience visiting classrooms, it is the classrooms where the students and teacher(s) meaningfully connect where the deepest learning takes place.

I'm someone who thrives with change. The idea of doing the same thing day in, day out is slow torture for me, and I knew it even in my first few years of teaching. When I began teaching in 1993, I was put in charge of four sections of English and social studies classes with three preps. I also was required to coach every season as well as complete such duties as covering arrival, lunch, recess, or dismissal. I loved every bit of it.

The biggest take-away from doing so much during a time when teachers were still expected to be involved in myriad ways outside of the classroom is that I became privy to seeing many sides of each student. I was able to watch Mike struggle with his writing yet excel behind home plate. I could support Lisa's last mile in the cross-country finals but also marvel at her ability to make connections between literary themes. I was able to understand when Rudy needed an extension on a homework assignment because his father was in town and hadn't been seen in months.

When students sense that their teacher knows them as people, amazing things can happen.

When students sense that their teacher knows them as people, amazing things can happen. New points of reference can be made. Casual banter can be informed by knowledge and understanding. New channels of communication can develop as the student arrives in class with a story about something the teacher knows means a lot to her. This knowledge is incredibly powerful. It reminds the student that the teacher is a human being, with interests to cultivate, time to manage, and goals to set and work toward. It makes the student feel not only better known, but remembered. The idea that a teacher saw his soccer game on Friday and referenced it on Monday, after an entire weekend, has an impact innately felt. Lastly, the student feels reaffirmed. His identity as a human being worthy of acknowledgment and appreciation is strengthened.

What results from this? The student knows his teacher has made a connection with him that is based on mutual respect and acknowledgment that he is an individual amongst a classroom of individuals. As far as how this impacts learning, it changes the dynamic from "doing school" to "doing something for someone who knows me." Students are on a path toward self-discovery. They want to be seen as distinct from who they used to be. A 5th grader doesn't want to be regarded as the same student he was in 2nd grade, just as a high school senior would shudder at being confused with his freshman self.

There is comfort to connection. Yet there also is power. This power comes by holding a mirror and reflecting back to a student that she acted within the parameters known about her or in opposition to those parameters. The student will respond to this mirror in a more accepting way if she knows that the teacher has taken time to go out of his way to see her outside of the classroom – to get to know a different dimension of her. For example, Scott, a 9th grader, came to me early in the year with a complaint when I was a principal. "I'm not being challenged. I thought English would be tracked honors and regular, and I'm in a class full of a wide mix of students."

I knew Scott. I had taken him to Boston as an 8th grader as part of a class trip, where he joined a 5am running brigade. I knew how graceful he was on the soccer field. I had read his writing and I knew he had a point about his strengths in both reading and writing. If he was challenging me about the velocity and trajectory of his freshman English career, he had a point.

I breezed through the perfunctory 9th grade doesn't matter – it's the last year to not worry about grades, that sort of speech. I then acknowledged that he has strengths in English. Weaknesses, too. And overcoming those weaknesses should be his focus over the next few years, since writing challenges don't get cleaned up overnight. He understood all of it. His body language indicated a willingness to leave. Message received.

But I wasn't done. Because I knew Scott over the years, I was able to acknowledge how I'd noticed his innate generosity toward others. I rolled off his closest friends to him, and I recognized that Scott seemed to thrive on their diversity. He nodded. "I didn't know you knew me so well," Scott said.

"The way I've seen you relate to your friends makes it clear to me that you will do the same for your classmates in that English class. Give them a chance to rise and to impress you. And help them out along the way. Remember, literary interpretation cannot be separated from life context. We bring ourselves into the way we interpret literature. Sit back and open yourself to the opinions of your peers. You might find yourself surprised at how much you learn from them."

Scott accepted this advice, and he even remembered this conversation long after it took place. In fact, 10 years afterwards. He and I were talking about career choices. He mentioned teaching, and he brought up this scenario. For Scott, it was a pivotal moment.

"I took your advice and I ended up learning more that year than in any other year before then. I learned from my teachers, but even more from my peers. That was a huge lesson. It taught me to get myself out of the way and to let others in."

Scott moved from his Brooklyn home to Los Angeles with a career change in mind. While successful as a young PR whiz, he feels a pull toward something more meaningful with long-lasting reward. In 2017, he joined the next generation of teachers who are eager to blend pedagogy with relationships.

Time to Pick a (Water Balloon) Fight

In *Connecting Brain Research with Effective Teaching*, Mariale M. Hardiman observes, "Learning is about connections. As educators, we see every day that the process of teaching and learning requires a connection between teacher and learner. This connective process, although interpersonal, is also neurobiological."[6]

To watch Rosalyn ("Ros") Won teach is to witness the power of connection in action. Whether setting off Alka-Seltzer rockets or turning her classroom into a news studio reporting on the "Amazing Arachnids," Ros possesses infectious passion about science that centers around *the wonder of it all*. Now a 4th grade departmentalized science teacher at Episcopal School in Baton Rouge, Louisiana, Ros has used her 18 years of expert teaching experience to deepen the science curriculum and to engage in relational teaching. Ros is currently teaching three class sections comprising 50 very fortunate 4th grade science students. Ros speaks about connection through the lens of putting your ego aside and just getting into it. In this case, it meant getting into a water balloon fight and watching as her students viewed her askew at first but with greater respect afterwards.

"One of my responsibilities as a teacher is to teach the curriculum, but also to help nurture and establish within my students a good foundation, how to be a good human being, how to think about the world. There's a lot more out there than just you. For example, yesterday we had Field Day at school and it was a great, fun afternoon. One of the stations at Field Day was a water balloon toss, and the kids were all tossing the balloons at each other. All of a sudden, I turned around and I felt a water balloon hit me and I saw that

6   Hardiman, Mariale M. (2003), *Connecting Brain Research with Effective Teaching* (New York: Rowman & Littlefield Education), p.10

it came from one of my students! I picked up the water balloon and hit him back, and the next thing I knew I was in the melee.

"I was having fun, the kids were having fun, and it was awesome. I thought, *All right, yeah, we're all going to get wet, but it is a hot day and the expression on the kids' faces is well worth it!'*

"We moved to the next station, and I heard a student from the other 4th grade section shout out, 'Ms. Won gets it!' I turn around, and that 4th grader, whose teacher didn't want to get into the water fight himself, is smiling at me with the widest grin of affirmation I've ever seen."

It's one thing to cheer on the faculty,

> The students are always watching, and when they come across a teacher "being real," they pay careful attention.

to make up cheers and remain in the stands. It's another thing to expose yourself to the "melee" and "get into it" and have fun. The students are always watching, and when they come across a teacher "being real," they pay careful attention. Being part of something silly, humorous, and playful means stepping out of your adult role. Yet the message is a powerful one: *I may be a grown-up, but my spirit retains the fire of childhood.*

Ros Won

While visiting Ressu Comprehensive School in Helsinki, Finland, I could hear the joyous background sounds of children playing outside the open windows. There's nothing that gives more of a sense of place in a school than peals of laughter, squeals, and the rhythmic beats that various games entail.

While completing my interview with Leena Liusvaara, the Principal of Ressu, I remarked, "It's really amazing to see how naturally the substance of our conversation (about student engagement) resonates. Not just cognitively, but from the heart, too. What I also love is just hearing the kids throughout this conversation in the background. That has been awesome. They're out there; they're playing and making noise. It's controlled chaos. It's the best."

Leena peered outside and observed, squinting, "There's some kind of game going on. I think there was some kind of water balloons, or something, with the 8th graders. It's fine. They can water themselves today!"

> Brain research supports the notion that a positive emotional climate paves the way for higher levels of learning and performance. On the other hand, a threatening, stressful learning environment can significantly impede learning.

Hardiman writes about positive emotional climates, such as the ones generated by Ros and encouraged by the Principal of Ressu Comprehensive School. "Brain research supports the notion that a positive emotional climate paves the way for higher levels of learning and performance. On the other hand, a threatening, stressful learning environment can significantly impede learning."[7] We will delve deeper into the subject of positive psychology later, but, for now, it's important to note that positive school environments foster deeper learning in students.

Time to Dance the Dance

Another way relational teachers connect with students is by learning about their interests while also sharing their own. Sometimes it only takes knowing one major passion that makes a student tick, and that one area can become a conversational topic throughout the entire school year. As teachers, we

---

7   Hardiman, Mariale M. (2003), *Connecting Brain Research with Effective Teaching* (New York: Rowman & Littlefield Education), p.23

notice and track areas of growth in our students and in ourselves. Therefore, if a student is passionate about a sports team, a teacher need only remember which team it is (and if a Boston Red Sox fan, you'd better be 100% certain!). Then the year ahead rolls out with moments to return to the Red Sox by asking about how the team is currently doing, who's being considered for next season, whether anyone's on the injury list, and the like. All it takes is the recognition of one such area of interest for a student to sense that his teacher cares about him not just as a number in a class attendance list or a score in the gradebook.

Ros explains this very well when she shares, "It is important for students to discover their passions and their interests. One of my responsibilities as a teacher is to teach the curriculum, but another equally important one is to help nurture and establish a good foundation within my students. It starts with showing them what my interests are. For example, I love sports. My students all know this about me from Day One.

"It's a delicate balance, or dance, because there's half the class that just can't stop talking about sports and then there's half that's like, 'Really? I could not care less about this.' One way for me to be a connective teacher is to make connections with all my students like, 'Okay…these other kids, what are they into? Is there some way that I can connect with them and also feel authentic?'"

As we will discover later, emotions play a large role in learning. Feeling connection is akin to feeling closeness. Whether that closeness is based on intimacy, understanding, or love, the underlying theme is connection-building

Connection and relationship-building result in validation.

and its corollary, relationship-building. According to Ros, connection occurs when students are given opportunities to relate to their teachers. Whether tossing water balloons or sharing passions for the Boston Red Sox, connection-building is nothing to overlook.

Ros concludes with a final example about the dance to connection – this time through an example involving actual dance. "I've been trying to keep up with the latest dance moves or Top-40 songs and I'm finding it to be increasingly more challenging as I get older. I said to my students, 'I have no clue about the Nae Nae!' But my students, they have taught me a lot. They responded, 'It's okay, Ms. Won. This is how you do the Whip and the Nae Nae…and the Quan and the Dab!' And they're helping me like it's as important as my lesson on the planets. And I realize that this is their effort to reciprocate. And through reciprocating, I am recognizing their efforts and validating them as people."

Connection and relationship-building result in validation. The time Ros took to learn these dance moves and to familiarize herself with the music worming into the ear canals of her students adds a tone to the classroom environment that fosters growth, authenticity, and (in many cases) joy.

Time to Mail the Letters

I spent many summers working as an overnight camp counselor at Camp Becket in the Berkshire Mountains of Western Massachusetts (there will be more on the significance of overnight camp to relational teaching – using Becket as a model – in the chapter, "Time to Have a Chat"). I wrote and read a lot of letters that were resurrected recently when clearing out my parents' house. These yellowed letters are relics of a time nearly forgotten, a time before the immediate ease of instant-messages. They were handwritten, revealing the personality of the writer. Sifting through these stacks of letters reminded me that connection is forged through writing.

Every year, Ros would have her students write a letter to themselves. What resulted was more significant than the letter itself.

"I started this tradition in my first year of teaching when I was a homeroom teacher. At the end of the year, I have my students write a letter to themselves as an 18-year-old. This letter contains reflections on the year. I say to them, 'Okay. You're going to write a letter to yourself. You may use it to reflect on memories, but maybe you might want to ask some questions as well.' We always have fun because they'll ask, 'Oh, so do I have a girlfriend now? What college do you think I'd be going to? Do I still have my same best friend?' All of these questions are great because it's about looking to the wide open future as it connects to their very real present."

Yet the exercise does not end there. Ros would hold onto the letters for years – until her students were graduating from high school. After all of the years in between, these students would receive the letters they'd written to themselves as idealistic children…and they would be deeply moved. This exercise stems from the fact that Ros' favorite teacher is someone she remains in touch with – 35 years after being a student in her elementary school classroom. "I just love the connection that I've had with her in my life when I was a kid and that I still have a connection with her to this day." Implied in that "love" is a sense of gratitude for the stability that comes with such a sustained teacher-student connection. We will discuss stability in the chapter, "Time to Find the Ballast."

There is something immensely gratifying that comes with receiving a letter, yet when it comes from your former self, this can be an unnerving experience, as we shed skins throughout our lives. This is most pronounced during the adolescent years, as self-identity becomes realized and the process of individuation begins.

Since 2016, Jennifer ("Jen") Dohr has been an English teacher at The Archer School for Girls in Brentwood, California. Over the past 25 years, she taught at several schools, including Harvard-Westlake School in Los Angeles, California. To walk into Jen's classroom is to walk into an intensely engaging learning environment. Student risk-taking is *de rigueur* in Jen's classroom, as is the assurance of steady growth in both mind and spirit.

In one of our conversations, Jen shared an incredible example of how a letter-writing exercise forged a close connection based on trust (the next chapter, "Time to Trust", is centered on the importance of trust in relational teaching). "A few years ago, we were studying *The Things They Carried*, by Tim O'Brien, and we had read the opening story, about the things the young American soldiers brought with them to Vietnam – both literally and figuratively. I handed out a piece of school stationery and a matching envelope just to elevate the assignment a bit. I know it's a bit of a gimmick, but we teachers do that at times! The students said, 'Wait – we're writing a letter? There are letters in this book... What's going on?'

"I responded, 'I want to know what you carry. It could be a necklace like the one I'm wearing now. My father gave me this. It's really important to me. I carry this necklace by wearing it around my neck. In that way, I carry the spirit of my father. So what do you carry? What could be in your stinky soccer bag right

> You could seal up an empty page of stationery, and I will never know, because this assignment isn't about me. It's about you.

now – this bag you're carrying that truly does stink, yet perhaps the cleats inside mean something to you...'

"Anyway, then we get into the abstract. 'Are you carrying not only love but pressure from your father? Are you carrying a sense of shame, of guilt, of over-the-top pride? You get the picture. So I want you to write tonight what you carry. It can be abstract, it can be concrete, it can be a mixture of both. You are to walk into class tomorrow with your letter sealed in its envelope.'

"Then the expected question is asked: 'Wait a minute. If the envelope is sealed, how will you know that we did the assignment?' I answer that I won't. 'You could seal up an empty page of stationery, and I will never know, because this assignment isn't about me. It's about you. It's about your having a chance to express yourself.'

"And they did it. They came in the next day. All they had to do was hold up a sealed envelope and honest to God, I could not tell if there were any words in there. Some students shared a little bit about what they wrote. None of the envelopes were opened. They could choose to mail it, to deliver it to me or not, to store it in their backpack, or to throw it away.

"Which brings me to Jasper. At the end of the year, we were completing a course evaluation, and it was Jasper who shot his hand up when I asked the class about the most memorable moment or assignment of the year. Jasper of the D+ on his end-of-year final, Jasper whose output never came close to matching what I was certain was his potential. Jasper shoots his hand in the air and he says, 'It was that assignment from when we wrote the letter, and you said you would never know if we did it, and we all got homework credit because it was like you trusted us.'

> When I give you feedback or when you're missing the bar, my belief in you remains unconditional. It's still there.

"That's all he said, and that's all he needed to say. It was such a profound moment for me as a teacher. It wasn't like I trusted him. I did trust him. Here you have this young man who's struggling and doesn't think he's good enough, and maybe that's what he needs, more of that message of 'I trust you'. Maybe that's connected to 'you can do this'.

"I had to trust Jasper to fail, too. I'll never know if Jasper wrote that assignment. But what he will hopefully remember for the rest of his life is, 'I was fourteen, and I was messing up, and most days I came to class without doing my work. I was shooting myself in the foot, and along came this teacher who allowed me to do that. So now it's on me if I fail; that's what I'll have to live with.' That message is more powerful than any grade.

I shared with Jen that this is a powerful story of unconditional trust and positive regard. It's about belief. *As a teacher, I believe that you can hit this bar, that you can spread your wings widely. That's the constant from me to you. When I give you feedback or when you're missing the bar, my belief in you remains unconditional. It's still there. And that fact is proven by my observing that you're not hitting the mark like I believe you can.*

Ms. Anneliese Euler is a high school and college theatre teacher in Los Angeles, California. I have had the privilege of watching her act on the stage for many years, in varied roles. She is a *force majeure*. While watching her teach, I was awestruck by her ability to tap into her students' youthful creative energy and channel it into something substantive. Part of her effectiveness is rooted in vivid memories of her own experience as an adolescent. In one of our several interviews, Anneliese recalled the power of the letter-writing exercise from her own adolescent perspective as a student.

"It was my sophomore year biology teacher. Every time I tell this story I still feel deep emotion. The assignment was to list everything we liked about ourselves. She gave us a blank sheet of paper and long chunk of writing time. Then she collected them with a promise to mail them to us five years later (which she did). I vividly remember how hard it was at first to keep coming up with positive traits, and how good it felt to get on a roll and come up with a long list. I folded it up so small when it was time to turn it in. It was a psychic antidote to the harshness I felt steeped in at the age of 16.

"I've long understood that being a student is a profoundly vulnerable thing, that when we enter a learning environment we subconsciously beg for confirmation or denial of our deepest hopes and fears. Our starting position is more or less, *Whatever the teacher says and does, I will take to mean that I am good, or bad; that I am smart, or stupid, that I am seen, or invisible.* And this stance is generally unconscious, especially for younger children, but I don't think it's that different for adults. The more I teach, the more I respect the reality that my job comes with serious spiritual responsibilities. I'm working inside the crucible of the human spirit. Because of this, teaching is a holistic, protean, intimate process. I am the one surfing this wave – with a mere 20 to 30 sensitive souls in my charge."

> The more I teach, the more I respect the reality that my job comes with serious spiritual responsibilities. I'm working inside the crucible of the human spirit.

The plane of memory brings Anneliese back to that example in vivid tableau. Here's a science teacher at a secondary school outside Boston in 1987 who had the gumption to stop the train and decide, *you know, this letter-writing exercise is more important right now. I see the challenges of growing up and I feel the pain they are feeling and I spot how they are coping with it because there's no escaping it.* This ability to empathize with one's students is critical to relational teaching. Sometimes the act of seeing your student and meeting her where she is at that moment can have profound effects on that student's sense of self.

Whether the envelope is mailed years and years after the letter is written or whether it is not opened at all is not the point of these three examples of letter-writing and relational teaching. The point is about connection made stronger in both cases. In Ros's case, the relationship was extended over the years and reignited upon receipt of the letter at the student's high school graduation. In Jen's case, the relationship was strengthened by the trust that she would not open the letter because the contents were assumed to be sensitive and deeply personal. In Anneliese's case, the empathy toward the adolescent experience demonstrated by her science teacher resulted in closer connection that remains with her today. In all three examples, the teachers connect with the humanness of their students: joy upon being remembered after so many years and confidence that their feelings are "OK." The power behind such connections is felt through the exercise of writing the letter… and what happens next.

Time to Tell Stories

Research supports storytelling's effectiveness as a teaching tool. It makes sense, given that we are social animals whose ancestors depended on storytelling to communicate cultural norms, share information about survival, and bond with each other. In the classroom, storytelling serves a similar purpose. Because learning is both cognitive and emotional, it makes sense that effective lessons contain stories. Students are always asking about the relevance of a lesson to their lives. Stories can communicate that relevance in a compelling way.

> Students are always asking about the relevance of a lesson to their lives. Stories can communicate that relevance in a compelling way.

Todd Whitten, a 20-year high school history teacher at Burlington High School in Burlington, Massachusetts, has spent half of his career in independent schools and the other half in public schools. Armed with a master's degree in political science and born with an unquenchable passion for history, Todd is wisdom personified in the classroom. His intellectual might is matched by a lighthearted humor that's generated by being in the presence of students. He is relaxed, affable, challenging, and spontaneous – all qualities that contribute to his teaching expertise. Todd and I discussed the importance of stories as tools for connection over a game of tennis when, between serves and volleys, he relayed a story about one of his students.

"So Jack says, 'You're the only class I like.' I respond, 'That makes me both happy and sad. Why is mine the only class?' 'Because you tell stories in class.'

But I know that's not the reason I'm his favorite class. It's because I know him. He is recognized for who he is.

"That said, I do tell a lot of stories in my class. It's the only way of keeping history alive and the students engaged!"

Todd uses storytelling in the classroom in ways that are quite different. For Todd, storytelling is a way to "make history come alive." Todd is the antithesis of the stodgy history teacher who relies on the same lecture notes he's been using for decades. Todd's classroom is dynamic and creative. Students are often in small groups working on projects and debating ideas. Todd adds levity and expert teaching efficacy by layering stories into the class lesson.

The idea of telling a story seems simple enough. Get a hook, find a message, make sure structure is at the core and characters are given flourishes of detail. Yet story is much more than its format. Genuine storytelling involves soulful communication. Autobiographical storytelling defines vulnerability. It takes a lot for someone to open up and reveal themselves in front of an audience. When that audience is a classroom full of hormone-laden, opinionated young people with under-developed prefrontal regulation, well, that's an even greater challenge.

Middle school history teacher and writer Chip Williams has spent his decades-long teaching career both at Learning Works Charter School in Los Angeles, California and at Cani Basari School in Canik, Turkey (currently closed by President Erdogan). Chip artfully navigates his classroom with authenticity, humility, and hope. His ability to empathize lies at the heart of his effectiveness as an expert teacher. Chip's gift for storytelling was revealed over tacos on Olvera Street on a mild September afternoon in Los Angeles, California.

> As long as I demonstrated interest in the subject, the students would perk up and become engaged as well.

"As long as I demonstrated interest in the subject, the students would perk up and become engaged as well. At times, I would replace some of the prescriptive reading assignments with some stories I grew up with. These were interesting stories told at a level they could understand. My stories would come from my lived experience. I talk about my travel experience. I bring in etymology from the different languages I've studied. What I shared in the classroom would come from life – from lived – experience." Students are attracted to autobiographical stories told by teachers that reveal challenges, achievements, and discovery. Such stories help students bond with their teacher. Chip's instinct about this was spot-on. The fact that he deviated from the script but not from the subject matter is noteworthy, as it was a way for him to communicate his material in a more relatable way.

"By telling my lived stories, I was able to take the prescribed material and massage it through stories about my lived experience. It's as if all this material becomes crystalized and shared by its being squeezed out to make the students rub it in – condensed – like a balm." In this way, Chip makes the intangible tangible. He takes the information and shapes it into something that is not only physical, but also healing.

Stories told from a teacher to her students are more than "entertainment." They are exercises in building empathy, and immensely effective ways to communicate a lesson through connection.

The idea of information being associated with healing or soothing is not often discussed. But it makes sense, given how the stories fire up the mirror neurons in the brains of the audience. When listening to stories, empathy is elicited. If a protagonist is inspiring to the audience, the brainstem will become activated with feelings of inspiration. In this way, one's biology and sociality are completely intertwined. When Chip imparts information through stories that elicit a mirror response, he channels not only the cognitive in his students, but the emotional as well.

Neuroscientist Dr. Mary Helen Immordino-Yang is an Associate Professor of Education, Psychology, and Neuroscience at the University of Southern California in Los Angeles, California. Her research centers on finding the emotional essence of learning, and her most recent book is titled, *Emotions, Learning, and the Brain*. In a TED Talk, Immordino-Yang speaks about the brain's response to storytelling.

"We do not learn neck-up like we're teaching to a classroom of empty buckets…we live socio-cultural, not just biological. The reason our socio-cultural environment is so powerful is because we feel the implications of those stories on the same neurosystems that keep us alive. The systems that keep us alive are housed, controlled, and felt by the same neural systems in our brain (as the socio-cultural). Social and biological survivals are tied together. Therefore, story elicits empathy – determination, smarts, grit…we generate inspiration through story."[8]

Neuroscience is just beginning to prove that stories elicit reactions from the listener as if the listener were actually inside the story. This "mirroring effect" is innate to our biology. This discovery speaks to our human drive toward empathy, and helps explain how story impacts the listener both cognitively and emotionally. Stories told from a teacher to her students are more than "entertainment." They are exercises in building empathy, and immensely effective ways to communicate a lesson through connection.

The Reverend Andrew Barnett, the Associate for Music and Worship at Cathedral School for Boys in Washington, DC, defines how storytelling bonds the connection between teacher and student. When storytelling takes a central role in the classroom, "the false dichotomy of 'I'm the teacher, you're the student' is broken. Instead, it's replaced by, 'we are on a journey together.'"

Aristotle stated, "Those who educate children well are more to be honored than they who produce them. For these only gave them life, those the art of living well."[9] This understanding speaks to the broader, relational, hidden curriculum brought into the classroom by expert teachers. The "art of living well" can be defined as the ability to witness the complexities of the world, while looking inward to review how the outer world is being processed and understood by the self. With this in mind, the responsibility of the teacher comes from knowing how to authentically reach his students through exposing his own spin, sharing his own concerns, expressing his passions, and stepping into the shoes of his students through the power of story.

Time to Empathize

Harper Lee's *To Kill a Mockingbird* remains one of the most popular assigned books in high schools today. For over fifty years, this coming-of-age story about a race-based trial told through the point of view of the 9-year-old daughter of the defendant's attorney has touched the minds and the hearts of generations. The book's effectiveness at communicating the power of empathy could only work through touching the heart and the mind of its reader. Just as with learning, reading also is both a cognitive and emotional experience.

I was required to read *To Kill a Mockingbird* during the summer before my 8th grade year. From the moment I started, I could not put it down. I was fascinated by the world presented through Scout's eyes. It was a childhood world already tugging at my burgeoning sentimentality. As a soon-to-be

8   https://www.youtube.com/watch?v=85BZRVE6M0o
9   https://www.goodreads.com/quotes/30782-those-who-educate-children-well-are-more-to-be-honored

teenager, I was experiencing bittersweet feelings of both excitement about my future adult life and remorse that my childhood would soon be gone forever.

I began 8th grade by taking a "did you read this" test in my first English class of the year. I remember thinking about the lack of value such an assessment held for me. You cannot reduce a novel containing such scope to 10 multiple choice questions. Surely we would be discussing the book tomorrow, I optimistically thought to myself. When tomorrow came, I remember receiving my 10/10 quiz. I also remember receiving a shiny new copy of Steinbeck's *Of Mice and Men*. We were required to "please open to Page One". Atticus, Scout, Tom and Boo Radley would remain in the rear-view mirror until I received a new shiny copy of *To Kill a Mockingbird* 15 years later. I was hell-bent on teaching that book to my class of 22 8th graders, and I was not going to allow such a literary suitcase of lessons on empathy pass them by.

Sure, these lessons were most likely "learned" through just reading the book. But my youthful teacher-self (who knew the passages to isolate, the character arcs to showcase, the subtleties in language that only Harper Lee could provide) knew that these students deserved something more. So after six weeks of annotation-based close reading, creative writings, and searches for themes and red herrings, my first English class came together with a bond that lasted throughout the school year.

Creating a world of empathetic learners is at the heart of my vision for why I teach.

When I look back today on why I felt such a burning drive to not merely assign but to *teach* this book, I think about the lessons on empathy that this story conveyed. "You never really understand a person until you consider things from his point of view ... until you climb into his skin and walk around in it." says Atticus to his daughter. Upon reading this line, I immediately think about my sister who has special needs and how much I wished growing up that everyone could empathize with her. There was sympathy toward her, yet in order to truly respect my sister Lin, empathy would be needed. Creating a world of empathetic learners is at the heart of my vision for why I teach. I acted upon it during my first class of 8th grade English students, and I continue to do so today whenever I can in my role as an administrator to middle school students. I have a framed movie poster of *To Kill a Mockingbird* in my school office, and I have referred to it dozens of times when I've had students in my office for disciplinary reasons.

Teaching empathy is not only relegated to an English class. Suzanne Buck, Head of School and Rector at Chatham Hall School in Chatham, Virginia, is a great source of positive reinforcement whose demeanor permeates her pores and defines her reputation as a relational school leader.

While we were talking about student engagement, Suzanne, stressing the need for fostering empathic connections in all subject areas, said, "Expert teachers help kids discover the personal connection they have to what they teach. For example, just last week I met with every department for an hour-and-15-minute meeting. It was kind of time-intensive, but it was wonderful for me to hear commonalities in different departments and hear what each department was concerned with or about. One of the things that were amazing to me was that all of our teachers – in every department were talking about empathy.

"I was hearing them talk about empathy in English, in terms of understanding the experience of a character, understanding the experience of an author, getting in an author's head. In history, the teachers were talking about empathy in regards to understanding what was happening at different time periods, the political environment and the economic environment in terms of geography and the people's experience. I was hearing them talk about empathy in math, in terms of thinking about how do our students help each other

> I was amazed. They were talking about empathy in all academic departments – not just the social sciences.

and support each other through solving a proof? How do we think about math collaboratively, so that all participants can engage in a meaningful way and understand the strengths and weaknesses of each other? I'm hearing them talk about empathy in the arts, talking about acting, embodying a character. In painting and photography, two different teachers were talking about relationships and relating to something different and presenting that experience through an art form, like observational experience.

"I was amazed. They were talking about empathy in *all* academic departments – not just the social sciences. To me, that speaks to spirit and educating with spirit, and freely thinking and contemplating spirit." Indeed, hearing Suzanne speak so passionately about the power and necessity of empathy in healthy classroom cultures brought me right back to my own years as a teacher when my eyes observed the eyes of my students as they followed the words on the pages describing the eyes of the young Scout with empathy – the central trait of human connection.

Time to Sidebar

When I was growing up, the most valuable lessons I learned from my father took place on our 22-foot catboat, *Solution*. He and I would sit at the helm, facing forward. He managed the tiller while I handled the sail. Staring over the far distances ahead, scouring for the next marker to orient our route, we would spend hours talking in a low-key manner about any topic that entered our minds. Occasionally, these meanderings would be punctuated by a "big ticket" topic – one that would seem intrusive in any other context, yet somehow wove into the conversation with relative ease while on the boat. Throughout my teenage years, Dad and I would have our deepest talks on *Solution*. These talks while sailing encouraged me to share my thoughts and feelings in a safe space with open ears and wide acceptance. There was no eye contact, given that we were facing forward, side by side, as we peered through our sunglasses. But I knew that I was being heard, and that's all that mattered.

> Students know when a conversation has gone well, and the effort made by the teacher to connect is often appreciated and remembered.

In school, we don't have the luxury of endless time to connect. Yet we do have opportunities that can provide a similar benefit. Whether it's sharing a walk down a hallway with a student, stopping by her table at lunch (tricky but possible!), or interacting with a student in the bleachers at a school game, such brief moments that occur throughout the school day provide important moments for a brief connection. In the words of Thomas ("Tom") Keller, Middle School Director at Sierra Canyon School in Chatsworth, California, "Just yesterday, I made real inroads with a student. I saw her in the breezeway alone. She asked if we could talk about her recent test and I responded, 'Let's definitely talk, but I've got to go down here. Can you walk with me?' And it happened so spontaneously...I gave her feedback in a 30-second sound bite. We were walking together. No eye contact, just listening. Moments like that you've got to always be prepared for."

Tom adds, "It could be that you have a student that you've struggled to connect with, but then the second you take them out of the classroom they're different with you. You know, you're not in a classroom, so it's a different type of conversation. And it can be like sitting out on the plaza at lunch even though you don't have lunch to eat. You catch the student in the plaza just so you can chat – and connect – in a non-threatening way."

Connection happens best in safe environments, as students are highly attuned to nuance and perceptions of threat. This is not to advocate being timid while approaching students for a quick chat; they can smell fear as well. Rather, by being aware of setting and tone, teachers can make deep inroads with individual students in just a few minutes. Students know when a conversation has gone well, and the effort made by the teacher to connect is often appreciated and remembered.

Tom continues, "So I think it is taking those opportunities when they arise, whether it be to go and chaperone something or watch part of the debate tournament, you kind of have to force yourself to do those things to get some connections with the kids."

Sara Bailey, a middle school English teacher at Francis W. Parker Charter Essential School in Fort Devens, Massachusetts, maintains a youthful exuberance and a reputation for helping students make huge strides in writing.

Sara reflects, "I think about the times when you need to have a sidebar conversation with a student. When you've built that rapport, these conversations can be smooth. I typically start with an open question like, 'So, how are you doing?' and then I just wait. You have to be comfortable with the open-ended question and very comfortable waiting for whatever answer results, when it comes. By doing this, you show each student you care, that you are a person to me. Over time, the 'How are you doing?' question feels less threatening and more curious. The students begin to settle in with you, to know that you're trustworthy and that you're just trying to connect. They know that I'm wanting to know just where they are now.

> It's important to keep an eye out for these relaxed moments when there is no spotlight shining and no 'correct' answer.

"For example, I had a student who moved into a new grade mid-year. During the entire spring, I kept trying to make inroads with him in class. I would ask questions, solicit his direct feedback, to no avail. The poor guy was 13 years old and at a new school and here was this teacher hounding him to connect! But at the end of the year, I saw him in the hallway and congratulated him for his successful basketball season. In response, he flat out said, 'I know I cared way more about basketball than school this year. Next year's going to be different.' The fact that he could say that and in 10 seconds share what needed to shift and how he planned to shift it…that's pretty amazing." What's also amazing is that it only took 10 seconds for Sarah's impact to resonate with her student – even after teaching him for an entire year comprised of thousands upon thousands of 10-second moments.

It's important to keep an eye out for these relaxed moments when there is no spotlight shining and no 'correct' answer. And when the moment comes, it's about being open to whatever answer is revealed. Finally, it's about knowing not to prolong the interaction. These micro-moments of connection can yield immense results, but they only occur when a teacher has the time to be open to them.

There are thousands of micro-moments that occur during the school day, and each one informs our moral, ethical, and attitudinal development. Strongly relational schools pay attention to the importance of these moments.

Jamie Neilson is the Upper School Director and English teacher at The Episcopal School of Los Angeles, California. A writer himself, his ability to depict character and context as it pertains to teachers, students and schools is incisive. For example, Jamie views hallway connection as linked to ethical growth. He sees these clustered, crowded areas as locations where students watch and learn from other students and teachers. However, he fears that technology appears to be impacting those serendipitous moments of contact. He explains, "The inclusion of technology in schools has begun to blur some of the ethical parameters that we have operated under, largely those that arise when you brush up against other people all day long and you get your ethical compass calibrated as a result. I think now, because you can say anything you want to millions of people right away without even looking a single person in the eye, we are risking a loss of the community as ethical ecosystem."

While hardly a technology luddite, Jamie nonetheless identifies the importance of human interaction within school communities. He astutely notes that an important part of education is accessed outside of the classroom, when teachers and students are at their most informal selves. The notion of recalibrating our ethical compass with each "brush" against another person resonates with truth. There are thousands of micro-moments that occur during the school day, and each one informs our moral, ethical, and attitudinal development. Strongly relational schools pay attention to the importance of these moments. They foster time for students to be off their devices and on with each other, as those experiences inform the development of the spirit within all members of the community.

Jamie is justified in noticing that teachers are challenged in their ability to sidebar not only by the timeless affect of moody adolescents but also by the tractor-beam grip of technology on those same students. It is impossible to sidebar when it feels like a struggle to pull students – and their eyes – from their devices and toward the sidelines. Yet it is always worth doing, even at the expense of an awkward moment, because on an intuitive level the student knows that he or she has been seen. Tom's wisdom and Sarah's example support the value of capitalizing on opportunities for a sidebar conversation.

Time to Set the Dinner Table

The dinner table presents a timeless image of connection. Like storytelling, the ritual of coming together over food has tribal roots. As social beings, we are motivated by the give and take of exchange that forges closer relationships. With food at the center, people take a seat within arm's reach, looking to satisfy their hunger yet also to feel a sense of inclusion. It is no surprise that the dinner table image came up repeatedly amongst the teachers I interviewed. The analogies to relational teaching are numerous. The dinner table involves preparation and execution, inclusion versus exclusion, and feeling cared for and embraced. It is a source of unexpected discovery, as conversations can meander into surprising areas. And it is about gratitude and respect, as demonstrated through manners.

The dinner table is a symbol of hospitality. One opens her home to welcome outsiders to her dining room table. This welcoming defines hospitality. Parker Palmer states, "Good teaching is an act of hospitality toward the young, and hospitality is always an act that benefits the host even more than the guest…By offering hospitality, one participates in the endless reweaving of a social fabric on which all can depend – thus the gift of sustenance for the guest becomes a gift of hope for the host. It is that way in teaching as well: the teacher's hospitality to the student results in a world more hospitable for the teacher."[10]

Alan Rivera, a 23-year world language teacher at The Park School in Brookline, Massachusetts, is beloved for his warmly relational approach to teaching. A photographer and avid traveler, Alan uses stories of his own travel to inspire students to "get outside" and explore. Alan has former students all over the world who have followed his edict to "get outside" and make a positive impact on the broader world. Many have returned to thank him for inspiring them.

10   Palmer, Parker (1998), *The Courage to Teach* (San Francisco: Jossey-Bass), p.51

When asked to describe his classroom environment, Alan replied, "In a way, it's almost like a big dinner table. We're all sitting, the desks are arranged like a dinner table, and everyone has their place. I will often say if the student is bumped out a little bit, 'Come join the table,' or 'Come join us.'"

This focus on inclusion is characteristic of all of the expert teachers with whom I met. The care that Alan takes to ensure that there are enough chairs for everyone reinforces a sense of belonging. Choosing to position his chair at the table with his students is about equality. Alan is not one of them; he is the teacher, while they are the students. However, he is absolutely one of them as a member of the school community. Alan's ability to teach while also noticing that a student may be "bumped out a little bit" shows that his attention is split yet not diluted. He re-invites that student back to the table by gently calling on him to "come join us."

> I will often say if the student is bumped out a little bit, 'Come join the table,' or 'Come join us'

Alan continues, "I feel like there's this sense of shared purpose when you sit at a dinner table with your family, everyone's around the table and your purpose is to eat a meal with them and to talk with them and to ask people questions, to tell a joke and to ask about their day, whatever you do at the dinner table. It's the shared experience of everyone doing it together, and you hope that people at the table will like your food and that they'll ask for more, and that they'll be polite and they'll know the social expectations of what we do at the table, and if they don't, you tell them because you want the experience to be a good one for everyone at the table."

Dinner table manners, like classroom norms, are cultivated and reinforced. Even if the food isn't to one's liking, a well-mannered guest will be polite. Even if today's lesson isn't to one's liking, an included and therefore valued student will be respectful because the student would want the experience to be a good one for everyone.

Alan concludes, "That's what my classroom is like. We're all at the table, we're all going to be doing our French or our Spanish, and I want everyone to enjoy the experience. I'm like, 'I love it and I hope you like it too. If you don't know how to do it, I'll help you. You can talk with your neighbor. I really want you to like what I prepared for you. If you don't like it, I'm sorry. I tried. If you don't know how to be at the table and I notice it, I want to help you to be at the table in a better way.'"

A teacher's efforts to make a lesson engaging are rarely recognized by non-educators. Alan describes the emotional expenditure wonderfully by likening

Alan Rivera

a teacher to a dinner host who presumably spent hours trying to create a positive experience for everyone at the table. As mentioned earlier, manners are expected. Dinner guests are 'helped' to be more polite dinner guests, just like students in Alan's classroom are 'helped' to be better members of the classroom community.

Alan ensures that each student who walks through the classroom door sees that he or she has a place card at the proverbial "table" with their name on it. Each student is known by name and addressed by name with the proper pronunciation, and each student is welcomed. In today's multicultural world, name pronunciation is essential. "Names have incredible significance to families, with so much thought, meaning and culture woven into them," Rita Kohli, Assistant Professor of Education at University of California in Riverside, California says. "When the child enters school and teachers – consciously or not – mispronounce, disregard or change the name, they are in a sense disregarding the family and culture of the students as well."[11]

The pressure on a teacher to set up an optimal classroom learning environment is strong. What if the table she sets is incomplete? What if the food is cold?

Colleen Kyle is a history teacher at Lakeside School in Seattle, Washington who possesses not only a limitless amount of content knowledge, but also

---

11 https://qz.com/775492/what-minority-students-hear-when-white-teachers-mispronounce-their-names/

a keen ability to listen. When you speak with Colleen, you literally *hear* her listening! In our phone interview (I from rainy London, she from the rainy Northwest, both holding cups of hot tea while 5,000 miles apart), Colleen draws an analogy between having full cups at the table and learning. "My classroom strives to be a trusting atmosphere, and if you as a teacher assume goodwill regarding your students, you're rarely going to be disappointed. It's better to start with a full cup of goodwill than start with an empty cup." The teacher who starts the year with her cup full of goodwill will lay optimal groundwork for success. The teacher who doesn't fill her cup with goodwill might encounter issues of broken connection with her students. Broken connection has the potential to manifest into broken trust and diminished hope.

Meghan Elizabeth is an American-born teacher at Ressu Comprehensive School in Helsinki, Finland. A passionately devoted teacher to her class of 4th grade students, Meghan is a sharp observer of the differences between the U.S. education system and Finland's. After watching Meghan at school, she and I spent an entire afternoon conversing over *mustikkapiirakka* (traditional Finnish blueberry pie – to die for) at Academic Bookstore in Helsinki (one of the greatest, not only in Helsinki but truly the world).

> When the child enters school and teachers – consciously or not – mispronounce, disregard or change the name, they are in a sense disregarding the family and culture of the students as well.

Many times during our interview, Meghan channeled Brazilian educator Paulo Freire and Finnish education leader Pasi Sahlberg by emphasizing the importance of giving teachers the freedom to make decisions on curriculum and instruction. "In Finland," Meghan stated, "it's a two-way street (regarding learning between teachers and students). There are no politicians and corporations deciding what is in the curriculum. No one from the outside dictating that we should be teaching this or that. The clear message is, if you're not an educator then there's too many spoons in the soup (as they say in Finnish)."

Teachers not only need time to prepare and oversee dynamic, enriching, and memorable dinner table conversations, but they also should be given permission to invite whomever they want – and choose to deny an invitation to those whose positions usurp control (politicians, parents, technology and other outside corporate influences). It is the teachers who should run their own kitchens. Too often, teachers voluntarily leave the profession because they witness the most engaging element of their job (creating lessons and instructional delivery that stimulates) being usurped by people who have never managed their own classroom.

A final epicurean story about the importance of connecting with students comes from Alan Rivera and it takes place in a setting far removed from his optimal classroom.

"Here's a story," Alan says. "I was in France recently with these two students. We were at a restaurant, and Elle had the menu and there were specials on the board. She asked, 'Mr. Rivera, what is the fish special?' and I responded, 'It's monkfish, and it's in a citrus cream sauce.' Elle followed up with, 'what's that sauce going to be like?' I said, 'I can only tell you what the menu says. I don't know what it's going to be like.'

> The clear message is, if you're not an educator then there's too many spoons in the soup.

"Elle said, 'I don't like sauce on my fish.' I said, 'Well, you shouldn't get it because it has the sauce.' Then she said, 'Maybe I should try it.' At that moment, I saw an opportunity. I said, 'Elle, maybe you *should* try it. If you don't like it, you don't have to eat it. But we're not going to order you something else. If that's the choice you want to make, go for it and try it.' Elle says, 'Maybe I won't have that then because I don't like sauce on my fish.' Thinking the saga is finally over, I say, 'Okay.'

"So the waiter comes and she orders the monkfish! I'm thinking, *Right on! Good! This is what I want. I want to teach them to like trying new things.* The fish comes, and she's poking at it a little bit while eating it very gingerly. After some time, Elle looks at me and says, 'Mr. Rivera, I don't like sauce on my fish, but in France I do.' I thought to myself, *I've done my job. I have done my job.*"

And indeed he has. At this point, Alan and I are both laughing while understanding the intricate strategies that come into play while encouraging teenagers to try something they've never tried before. The removal of Elle's comfort zone was also a removal of the same-old, same-old for her.

Alan recognizes this, as he followed up this story with a reflection. "For Elle, and for me, that was a great moment. I feel like in some small way, I taught her not to be afraid of something different. Maybe I taught her that there's a whole world of things outside her realm of experience that she will love just as much as she loves that fish with sauce. That's huge for me. That's a huge source of affirmation." Thanks to Alan's relaxed encouragement, Elle chose to lean in to a new experience, and she found it to be alright – at least in a country thousands of miles away!

Time to Be 'The One'

Just as it can take just one conversation to turn a student around, or one optimal classroom environment to bond a diverse group of 30 students, all it takes is one *person* to change a life. When we look back at teachers who made a difference, chances are they possess the relational elements that serve as titles to the six chapters of this book. Yet when you consider just one person who made the greatest difference in your life, well, then you're entering a rarefied arena of superlative character, strong moral conviction, and simply serendipitous timing. That one person – a teacher, coach, neighbor, rabbi, camp counselor, or bus driver – is someone you can credit for inspiring, saving, or re-routing your life. That one person can often be found in schools, and he or she is not necessarily in charge of a classroom.

> All it takes is one *person* to change a life.

Dr. Jonathan Zaff, Executive Director of The Center for Promise, the research institute for America's Promise Alliance, housed at Boston University's School of Education in Boston, Massachusetts, is an extraordinary person whose organization is doing great work toward eradicating the U.S. dropout rate while also creating opportunities for those who are underserved.

Jonathan's message to me is simple yet precise. "You don't have to be everything to every student. But, everyone – the receptionist, the nurse, the teacher, the coach, anyone – can do something for each student. Together, these 'somethings' are what keep students in school." Indeed, this is proven time and again in his organization's research, which is full of student anecdotes regarding "the one person who told me I mattered."

Being "The One" is not something you can strategize or construct. It involves authentic connection and serendipity. In many cases, teachers don't know they are the one until the end of their relationship with the student.

Jen Dohr, the English teacher currently at The Archer in Los Angeles, California, tells an inspiring story about both being the one and finding the one. This story took place years ago, yet Jen remembers with such clarity that it seems as if it took place just last week.

"Sasha was coming to class day in and day out in 7th grade without her homework, but making interesting comments in class, so I was feeling really challenged by her. I finally got down on my knees to be at eye-level with her at her desk, and I asked, 'How can I help you? Is there something I can do better?' She looked at me and said, 'Well, maybe if you could just put your initials in my planner after I copy down the homework from the board – just to see if I got it right.'

"I was flummoxed. My initial thought (because I hadn't taught 7th grade in years) was, 'Wow, this feels like elementary school. She's asking me to see if what she has copied from the board is accurate?' But then I thought to myself, 'Meet her where she is, not where I want her to be.'

"Of course I said yes.

Everyone – the receptionist, the nurse, the teacher, the coach, anyone – can do something for each student. Together, these 'somethings' are what keep students in school.

And not one time all semester did she miscopy what was written on the board. Every time I put down my initials, what she had written was perfectly accurate. I could have taken the attitude that 'this is a waste of my time.'

"But I came to realize that the point wasn't really about checking that she could copy from the board correctly. The point was about making a connection with her. Over time, my initials on Sasha's planner changed to a little smiley face, which then changed to a short note, like 'How are you?' We developed an unspoken connection through her planner. She'd smile, and we would do this every single day.

"Sasha was still having a difficult time with assessments, so I thought I'd take our note writing a bit further. I started going over to her during tests while I was passing back papers (or pretending I was passing back papers) with a little sticky note under my thumb. I would write a different message on it every time, like 'Confidence!' or 'I believe in you,' or 'You can do this.' I would just stick the note on her test while she was taking it, and then walk away, and not act like I was treating her any differently from the other students.

"I'd go back and sit down at my desk while the students were finishing the assessment, and I would always catch Sasha's eye. She would look up at me with this huge smile as if to say, 'I saw that note, I know what you're doing to me. I know that you see me.' It was such a great example of the power of the unspoken connection."

As a coda to this beautiful story about the power of being seen as the essential core of teacher–student connection, Jen shared a video Sasha sent her at the end of the year. In it, Sasha is facing the camera in an empty classroom. She starts off by stomping her feet in rhythm and repeating phrases like, "Ms. Dohr, you're awesome!" and "You're the coolest, Ms. Dohr!" Her exuberance makes this part of the video stand out, although it's all somewhat generic…until the second half, when Sasha states, "Everyone loves you, especially me!" Then Sasha's voice grows deeper, as she continues, "Why? Because you helped me! With everything and everything more and everything else! That's why I love you, Ms. Dohr!"

You've got to meet the students where they are.

Sasha is a student who started off struggling so much in her 7th grade English class, yet she overcame her challenges – through discrete communication, care, and connection. Sasha spent most of the year coiling up at her desk, her inward body position communicating self-protection. Yet here she is at the end of the year, with her arms reaching out as far as possible, a wide smile, and radiant eyes. Her confidence is intact, her spirit is refueled, and her heart is openly sharing her gratitude for a teacher who was truly The One.

Time to Meet Them Where They Are

As research confirms, it is important for learners to find something personal in the material being taught. Emotions drive learning. If teachers make time to connect with their students in an individual way, they can then make the learning personalized so that it appeals to both the heart and mind. The notion of "meeting students where they are" is an empathic one. This approach demonstrates authenticity and embraces humility.

Andrew ("Andy") Chappell, the Director of Studies at The Roxbury Latin School in West Roxbury, Massachusetts, and a teacher with 20 years of experience, shares a story about a 7th grade boy challenged by adjusting to this venerable school for boys.

"You've got to meet the students where they are. You can't expect kids to hit a bar that's impossibly high. For example, we took in a new 7th grade boy this year named Oscar. I knew Oscar was talented because I'd seen his testing scores. Yet he was not succeeding like he should. He was hiding his homework, he was avoiding in-class interaction. I teach one of his classes, and one day I saw he didn't have his homework all done.

"At the end of class, after the other kids had left, I quietly said, 'Oscar, can I talk to you? I noticed you didn't have your homework done. I'm disappointed, but I know you're struggling. Let's meet tomorrow to go over the material. We both know you can do this.' Oscar came from a large, urban public school and it was clear that he was still processing the culture and academic standards of our school. Yet it was important for me to build our relationship with the knowledge that with support he will succeed. Again, I know his potential. To get him motivated he needed to know that I'm interested in him as he adjusts to his new school."

Andy was gracious in his interaction with Oscar. Instead of calling him out, or addressing his concern in front of others, Andy waited until the other students had left. In a quiet voice, he expressed his concern. Yet he didn't treat Oscar pejoratively. Rather, he used the word "disappointed." It is far easier to have an authority figure say they are "disappointed" rather than "upset." One is disappointed when someone does something that's not common or consistent. One is upset when he feels pained personally. Oscar's actions don't impact Andy. They only (negatively) impact Oscar. Andy was aware of this, and he therefore expertly chose the term "disappointed" over "upset." In his approach, Andy was meeting Oscar "where he (was)." He replaced judgment with understanding. By doing this, he affirmed Oscar, and he defused what could have been a tense situation.

> I often ask myself the question, 'When they are 35 years old, are these kids going to be happy?

Andy also allowed time for both of them to reflect on and process the situation. Andy shared his observation; he didn't probe into it. Rather, he suggested meeting the next day, allowing time for emotions to subside and introspection to take over. The day's interactions and the next day's meeting will serve as first steps down a longer road of acclimation.

If Andy hadn't used his expert, relational teaching approach, the encounter might have veered off in a different direction. Often, when teachers feel a lack of time in their school day, they fall into the trap of instant, reaction-based feedback. Instead of allowing that to occur, Andy took a deep breath and opted for a long-term approach. Oscar is a better student for it, and Andy benefitted as well from making this sensitive inroad into the guarded and insecure soul in his care.

"When I view the students in my school," Andy shares, "I often ask myself the question, 'When they are 35 years old, are these kids going to be happy?' Schools can be amazing places to spend our growing years if they focus on getting kids to reach high levels of happiness and keep them there."

The storytelling high school history teacher Todd Whitten shares the same approach as Andy here. He views his role as connecting with students in order to instill optimism and hope about their futures. This comes with being noticed as an individual and the way he does it is to intentionally connect with each one of his students throughout the year, putting *life* ahead of *school*.

"I often try to sit down with my students individually, and just talk about life, not school. Definitely not school. It's always life: 'Tell me about your favorite movies.' 'What did you do this summer?' 'Do you have brothers and sisters?' 'What do you do outside of school? Do you do sports? Are you into theater? Who's your favorite sports team? What do you love about Boston?' All that sort of stuff that is not school, it's people."

> It is literally neurobiologically impossible to build memories, engage complex thoughts, or make meaningful decisions without emotion.

I asked Todd why it is important to ask these life-based questions, which can appear to be perfunctory or even invasive to the highly-attuned adolescent. His answer reminded me why relational teaching is so important an element of optimal classroom teaching.

"It's because very few adults do it with them. Students tell me they go through the entire day and nobody uses their name. Nobody says, '*Matt*, what do you think about that?' Teachers just point and say, 'Yes.' Or, 'Go ahead.' Many students sense that this is the norm. It's so depressing, but just that very act of saying, 'Matt, how's your day going?' is absolutely noticed and noted by the student. It is the emotional part of what we do every day and it impacts learning, for sure."

Recent brain research backs up what expert teachers already know: teaching and learning cannot be separated from emotions. Rather, teachers use emotion-based methods to instruct, assess, motivate, and engage students in the classroom every day.

In her excellent book, *Emotions, Learning, and the Brain*, University of Southern California professor and researcher Mary Helen Immordino-Yang states, "A revolution in neuroscience over the past two decades has overturned early notions that emotions interfere with learning, revealing instead that emotion and cognition are supported by interdependent neural processes. It is literally neurobiologically impossible to build memories, engage complex thoughts, or make meaningful decisions without emotion."[12]

Shawn Achor, a positive psychology guru, author of *The Happiness Advantage*, and creator and teacher of the popular *Happiness 101* course at

---

12 Immordino-Yang, Mary Helen (2016), *Emotions, Learning, and the Brain* (New York: W. W. Norton), p.18

Todd Whitten

Harvard University in Cambridge, Massachusetts, states, "Instead of narrowing our actions down to fight or flight as negative emotions do, positive ones broaden the amount of possibilities we process, making us more thoughtful, creative, and open to new ideas…and when positive emotions broaden our scope of cognition and behavior in this way, they not only make us more creative, they help us build more intellectual, social, and physical resources we can rely upon in the future."[13] Shawn's idea of a "broadening effect" brilliantly frames the impact happiness has on learning. Happy (i.e., content) people allow themselves to be open – to ideas, risks, and questioning. This information is then more confidently sculpted, analyzed, and synthesized.

Achor refers to the Greek term, *eudaimonia*, which he defines as, "…a contented state of being happy and healthy and prosperous – 'human flourishing.'"[14] The healthy classroom is the flourishing classroom. We visualize it with imagery much like an unfolding flower, or an old wall being stripped of its paint layers. Students and teacher experience *eudaimonia*, which centers not on manic joy but comforting and consistent contentment. In this state, the brain is relaxed. The self is "prosperous" in ideas, imagination, and potential.

In his book *Tribe*, author and journalist Sebastian Junger defines the self-determination theory as based on the premise that, "Human beings need three basic things in order to be content: they need to feel competent at what

13 Achor, Shawn (2010), *The Happiness Advantage* (New York: Crown Business: Crown Publishing), p.44
14 Ibid., p.40

they do; they need to feel authentic in their lives; and they need to feel connected to others. These values are considered 'intrinsic' to human happiness and far outweigh 'extrinsic' values such as beauty, money, and status."[15] Expert teaching requires time to foster these things to make a stronger classroom. Teachers need to maintain strong connections with individual students while also ensuring that students are connecting in a healthy way with each other.

> Positive emotions can actually contribute to long-term memory and higher-order thinking processes.

Positive connections such as the one forged between Andy Chappell and Oscar are at the heart of relational teaching. These expert teachers take time to cultivate these connections knowing that it makes a positive impact on students. Relational teachers like Andy recognize that the closer the connection a teacher is able to create with students, the higher he can hold the bar and the more confidently he can feel about classroom gains as a whole.

Mariale M. Hardiman sums up the impact of happiness on learning when she states, "Positive emotions can actually contribute to long-term memory and higher-order thinking processes. Researchers have found that laughter, for example, produces chemical changes in the brain and increases the body's production of neurotransmitters, which enhance alertness and memory and boost the immune system."[16] In order to create a sense of freedom to laugh in the classroom, an expert teacher connects with her students. Thus, as Meghan Elizabeth, the teacher from Ressu Comprehensive School in Helsinki, Finland, told me while sitting in her classroom of 25 ten-year-olds on the last day of school, "You can have the best lesson in the world, but if you can't connect to your students then nobody cares." Teachers need time to find the humor and to encourage space to share stories, be themselves, and laugh heartily. Their students' learning effectiveness depends on these abilities.

Recapping the Relational: Connections Count

Connections count. As human beings, we are driven toward social interaction. We instinctively value being part of a community. School is often the first community a young child enters into outside of the family home. Expert teachers recognize this, and they understand that learning is enhanced by

---

15 Junger, Sebastian (2016), *Tribe* (New York: Twelve: Grand Central Publishing), p.22
16 Hardiman, Mariale M. (2003), *Connecting Brain Research with Effective Teaching* (New York: Rowman & Littlefield Education), p.33

forged connection between students and teachers.

Connection is built through shared interest, such as sports and dance. It comes through putting yourself out there with the students (so if there's ever a water balloon fight in your school, the wise idea would be to join it and watch your status rise like a legend!).

Letter-writing exposes the personal and demonstrates connection through story. Strength presents itself through empathy, for example by teaching literature that touches the human spirit. I attended a lecture recently by a well-known puppeteer from the BBC here in England. The audience's brain was tricked into believing these inanimate objects were breathing, emoting and connecting with us. The same transference takes place with characters in literature and history, which are brought to life through connection-based relational teaching. Empathy is generated in disciplines outside the humanities, as explained by Suzanne Buck, when she stated that each of her departments mention empathy as the central concern in their teaching.

Taking the time to have a quick sidebar – even if just for 30 seconds – forges opportunity for connection. Difficult conversations are made successful through proper timing and pace. As Andy Chappell demonstrated, sometimes a core life lesson needs 24 hours to incubate before delivering to a student. When talking with a student, it is important to meet them where they are. If the conversation goes well, you might emerge as "The One" when the student looks back from age 35 and gives thanks toward the adult who truly saw them during their dark and challenging times. The classroom dinner table is set with thought toward inclusion. Relational teachers know that connection cannot be achieved when the seats aren't in optimal order with nametags properly spelled and food properly prepared.

As teachers, we know that the classroom rarely feels like a raucous dinner party, with animated conversation and chortling laughter and harmonic cacophony and guests unwilling to leave when the bell rings. However, we recognize that good things happen when students and teacher are seen buzzing and teetering on the cusp of chaos while focused on the subject matter. When everyone is in the flow and feeling like time is moving at double-speed and no one is asking to use the bathroom and the questions and answers are ricocheting from all directions, connection is taking place and true learning results. Those moments – infrequent yet cherished – help keep us in this profession another year.

Meghan Elizabeth

Time to trust

"It's always been a matter of trust."

Billy Joel

The relationship between teacher and student is based on learning expectations and predicated on trust. The more a teacher builds trust with their students, the higher the probability that students will learn. Yet trust-based connection is not achieved merely through being kind, engaging, or theatrical. While there is a place for acting in teaching, the deepest connections are formed through the exposure of vulnerabilities and honesty: the revelation of the true self. It is through being human that human connections develop.

Trust is a firm belief in the reliability, truth, or ability of someone (or something). As teachers, we are expected to model optimal social behavior. In *The Students Are Watching*, Ted and Nancy Sizer write about how teachers' behavior is deeply absorbed by students. Teachers are expected to model positive character traits of all types, yet trust is more than a trait. Trust is a characteristic, a value, an ethic, and a workable goal. Trust is a two-way connection between people, influenced by the stability of their virtue. Trust is delicate and complex. We grow up being told that "trust is earned over time," yet also "quickly broken."

What can we do if we teach in a culture where trust is not established or well-nourished? This can be due to an over-staffed administration looking to assert relevance through top-down initiatives, an administration perceived as weak when facing bullying parents, a teacher evaluation system driven by students' standardized test scores, or any number of other reasons. Whatever the reason, when trust is lacking, the classroom culture suffers and learning is negatively impacted. And in classrooms where teachers and students meaningfully trust each other, the deepest learning takes place.

> Teachers are expected to model positive character traits of all types, yet trust is more than a trait. Trust is a characteristic, a value, an ethic, and a workable goal. Trust is a two-way connection between people, influenced by the stability of their virtue.

Time to Be Like Finland

Ressu Comprehensive School (Grades 1–9) is located in Helsinki, Finland. It is a tuition-free school (as are all comprehensives in Finland) serving over 450 students from 35 nationalities. Housed in a well-maintained 80-year-old building that served as a hospital in the Second World War, Ressu's heart is found in another building located inside its gates: the red doghouse belonging to Snoopy, whose name in Finnish is "Ressu".

The joy conveyed through the Peanuts comic strip is emulated at Ressu Comprehensive, and the hallways buzz with the spirit of learning and the laughter of children. Ressu Comprehensive School principal Leena Liusvaara elaborates on the historical perception of teachers in Finland.

"If you go back in history, from the Middle Ages onwards, who was keeping the schools? It was the priest. Education would be from the church. In Finland, the two most important people would be the priest and the village teacher."

Renowned Finnish educator Pasi Sahlberg states that, "Today's Finnish education policies are a result of three decades of systematic, mostly intentional development that has created a culture of diversity, trust and respect within Finnish society in general and within the education system in particular."[17]

Today, Finland is known for its educational excellence. Every principal has been a classroom teacher, so administrators who have spent years in the classroom supervise teachers. Every teacher has completed a two-year master's program in instruction, pedagogy and subject mastery. The acceptance rates

---

17 https://www.irishtimes.com/news/education/how-finland-emerged-from-recession-with-the-best-education-system-in-europe-1.560673

at these graduate schools rival law and medical schools : 10–15%. Therefore, just getting accepted is an accomplishment in itself. Upon graduation, new teachers start their first year with the gift of trust received from Day One.

While researching the history and design of Finland's education system, I came across a comment from Shannon Frank, an American English teacher from Houston, Texas, who was visiting a number of Finnish schools for her own professional development. Shannon observed that "surprisingly, the word 'trust' was something we heard repeated so many times that it became an inside joke among our group. The Finnish education system is founded on the concept of trust, with a national curriculum much broader than Common Core or our state standards."[18]

Inspired by everything I'd learned about Finland and intrigued by the concept of a nation that trusts its teachers, I travelled to Finland to interview school principals, teachers, journalists, and parents. "Finland is a trusting culture on the whole; it shouldn't surprise anyone that we are trusting in our schools as well," said Katya Panzar, a writer and journalist in Helsinki, Finland, with whom I spoke. "Everyone rides bikes here, yet no one steals them." Meghan Elizabeth, the 4th grade teacher at Ressu, commented, "I was missing my bag – license, I.D., the whole gamut – and it was right where I left it, in a public space, untouched. You hear stories like this all the time here. There is a culture of trust."

The Finnish educational system promotes trust amongst its teachers from parents, administrators, students, and colleagues. Every teacher I spoke to mentioned that trust is a central concept in his or her school. Ilona Taimela, a history teacher from Ressu, states, "Finnish teachers are given a lot of autonomy. They have always been really respected and trusted."

In order to be fully autonomous in her classroom, a relational teacher relies on the principal's unconditional support. For example, Meghan was an American from Texas who wasn't planning on spending seven years (thus far) in dark, snowy Finland. Meghan has followed the path of many international educators in this globally respected country: she stayed.

A major factor contributing to Meghan's choice to remain is the freedom she has from her principal to explore new concepts and instructional methods. Inherent in such exploration is the risk of failure. Sometimes the lesson doesn't go as planned, a student will ask a question the teacher cannot accurately answer, or the lesson will unravel as it bridges theory and practicality. A good principal knows this, and will advocate for the teacher, even when she fails – or because of it.

18 http://blogs.edweek.org/edweek/global_learning/2016/03/an_american_teachers_thoughts_on_the_finnish_education_system.html?r=1145059607

Meghan explains, "I am allowed to fail in my job. My principal encourages me to fail. She'll say, 'Take a risk. Try something out. The worst thing that can happen is it's not very effective, or it doesn't work, and you will get immediate feedback. But then you've learned something and you know how to do it differently the next time.'" The trust that is engendered as a result of such support is priceless.

The school day is structured in a way that promotes collaborative trust-building among teachers. Students have a 15-minute recess every 45 minutes (and teachers use that time to recharge with their colleagues). The only required state-level standardized test is issued to 16-year-old students who are preparing for university. All other standardized tests are only used internally; they are never linked to teacher performance evaluations.

In Finland, teachers hold a respected position in society. Resources are given to teachers to work with students emigrating from all over the world, and accountability measures are de-emphasized. As a result, Finnish schools are trusted to create individualized teaching programs that result in optimal learning.

> The odds of someone...
> born below the poverty line
> becoming a middle-class
> adult are better in Finland
> than in almost any other
> country. More important,
> those odds are measurably
> better than they were 20
> years ago. And it's almost
> all because of the way the
> Finns changed their schools.

The payoff is greater upward mobility. *The Toronto Globe and Mail* international affairs columnist Doug Saunders writes, "The odds of someone...born below the poverty line becoming a middle-class adult are better in Finland than in almost any other country. More important, those odds are measurably better than they were 20 years ago. And it's almost all because of the way the Finns changed their schools."[19]

The Finnish education system has been resurrected over the past thirty years as a result of intensive focus on social mobility for all. Over this period of time,

19 https://beta.theglobeandmail.com/news/national/education/how-finland-is-fighting-inequality-with-education-andwinning/article29716845/?ref=http://www.theglobeandmail.com&

the population of Finland moved from being largely homogenous to broadly diverse due to an influx of immigrants not only from the European Union, but also from Russia, Estonia, and Somalia. As of late, asylum seekers from Iraq and Afghanistan also have found Finland.

On the topic of trust, Meghan states, "In the U.S., it's about lining up in single file, and metal detectors, and campus police, and hall passes, and all of this stuff which is designed to manage and control. That's not what they do here. It's an independence thing, and learning how to get from one place to another, and trust.

"I tell my students, 'I trust you to go from here to there, and if you don't, then I won't trust you the next time.' My trust is given and it's also reciprocated, such as when they say, 'Wow, my teacher trusts me to do this. She's giving me her keys to go and get my report from a printer all the way in the lab, and she trusts me to come right back.'"

I spent time in Meghan's class of about 25 students. Her class was globally diverse, with native-born Finns, as well as students from the U.S., England, India, and Somalia. Her students were vibrant, engaged, and full of joy. Meghan did very little class management. Granted, I visited on one of the last days of the school year; however, instead of being hyped up for summer, the students in Meghan's class were focused and content.

Finland provides a powerful example of trust-based relational teaching. The individual student approach by the teachers and extended team of educational experts is an example of truly never giving up on a child. As a result of this, and a curriculum that values collaboration and exploration over stress-inducing standardized testing, students remain in school and society benefits.

Time to Find the Ballast

As previously mentioned, I grew up sailing on our 22-foot catboat, *Solution*. I always found sailing on that wide-berthed coastal cruiser to be the best of all worlds because it heeled dramatically, yet it could never capsize. The design of the hull leaves the captain confident that no matter how challenging it is to find the ballast of the boat, he would never risk sinking the ship. In relational teaching, trust grows best in sometimes-dramatic yet ultimately stable environments. Once trust is established between teacher and student, engaged learning takes place.

Jen Dohr, the English teacher at The Archer School who assigned – but did not collect – letters students wrote to themselves, reveals the best advice she was ever given about teaching. This advice came from a beloved Head of School at the independent school where she taught for 20 years in Los Angeles, California. "One of my former Heads of School used to say, 'If students trust you, you can get away with murder.' In other words, if you show that you're fair, you're flexible, you're trustworthy, you can make mistakes, you can push them too hard, you can say you have to take back something you said the day before – because they really trust you."

It is worth repeating that trust is about stability. Students of all ages require stability to be open to learning. They seek it out even before they are able to speak. They know when an environment is unstable, and when a classroom feels like an environment where potentially negative surprises can occur.

The instability that defines a less trusting environment can be interpersonal. For example, Chloe, a middle school student from Boston, states, "I had the same teacher last year for three years. We have a connection because we've known each other for so long. This year, I have an English teacher who's complicated and I can't trust her day by day. Some days she'll be really nice to me, and some days she'll just get frustrated with me randomly. I don't really know how to handle it, because I don't really have an interest in English, either, so it's hard for me to connect with her. Yet unlike with other teachers, I don't want to try to connect because I don't know which personality I'm going to get when I do."

By exploring where trust can be broken, we can advocate that teachers need time to take that deep breath and manage their moods over the course of the school day. We are only human, and therefore vulnerable to the occasional building up and subsequent lashing out of emotions we regret expressing. We cannot be perfect all the time. However, we need to work in schools where the base value of time is considered. Most professionals can find a space to escape to that will provide an opportunity for them to take a deep breath and count to 10. Teachers rarely even have the time to use the bathroom during the course of the school day! Something needs to give.

Rebecca, a student from California, provides another example. "In an English class I am taking, we had to write memoirs. I wrote mine about when I was really little. I was sick – not a big deal, I'm better now. Anyhow, I wrote about being sick as a child, and then later in the year I told my teacher that I also have an eye problem that requires me to take an eye exercise and it's really annoying. She turned to me and she said, 'Wow, you sure have a lot of medical problems.' Everyone was silent. It was super awkward. And she's like, 'Sorry. That was probably inappropriate.' I was like, I didn't mind that much, because I don't mind talking about it. But it was something that was so inappropriate and so uncomfortable for everybody involved, that a teacher would bring something like that up that's so inappropriate in really any setting. It was weird."

Mariale M. Hariman states, "Discipline that embarrasses and humiliates students can downshift attention from the brain's thinking centers to its emotional centers."[20] This example really hit hard because of the magnitude of the lapse of judgment. No student deserves to be publicly shamed for his or her medical challenges. Chances are the teacher was stressed out and unable to find the time during the school day to regulate her emotions and find the ballast in herself. Chances are she regretted what she said later that day, or in the evening, or whenever she was able to find a moment to herself. Still, I am concerned about this student's overall experience in that class. There is no possibility for open and successful learning when one experiences broken trust by the authority figure in the classroom – the one who threw the ballast of the classroom off-balance and must now find the strength to right the ship single-handedly.

I would say it also kind of cuts the other direction too. The way a relational teacher handles the inevitable moodiness in most adolescents involves incredible nuance. Burlington High School history teacher Todd Whitten explains, "If a student is not having a good day, she is down, for whatever reason, it's understandable – she's a teenager, after all! But to have an adult say, 'Hey, are you all right? Are you doing okay today? You're not your usual self.' That action – that desire to connect – potentially shortcuts a whole bunch of classroom problems too, because I have connected with that student.

> Discipline that embarrasses and humiliates students can downshift attention from the brain's thinking centers to its emotional centers.

"For example, I had this one girl, Jessica, who was one of those kids who, *as she goes, the class goes.* She's a ringleader kid. If she comes in in a bad mood, boy you're going to have a rough, rough day. All the Christmas tree lights will start going off. So my job is to remove that one bulb before the other 29 start flickering out also. My approach with Jessica is totally tactical. At the beginning of class, when the kids are coming in and getting settled, I notice her. She comes in with a sulky demeanor and she's just like, 'Humph.' So I kill her with kindness, in a way. I approach her, 'Hey, what's going on? How are you doing today? Something's different.' I say something, anything. And in my years of teaching, I've realized that you can move a student's mood just by noticing that she's in a bad mood. By calling it out, she is going

20 Hardiman, Mariale M. (2003), *Connecting Brain Research with Effective Teaching* (New York: Rowman & Littlefield Education), pp.30–31

to perk up pretty much 90% of the time. It's not because you've embarrassed her – this is done discreetly – but it's because Jessica knows that somebody cared. This is huge, and as a result learning can happen."

Todd chuckles to himself as he reflects on this anecdote. "And if it doesn't work? Forget it. You're done." We both nod in agreement, visualizing the Christmas tree lights constantly flickering in the classroom and the teacher on the electricity-generating bike, spinning his legs in a feverish attempt to maintain their illumination. Sometimes that's exactly how teaching feels!

Time to Get Organized

Jen Dohr, the English teacher from The Archer School in Los Angeles who used unopened letters as a way to connect, elaborates on another type of trust that is required to build an optimal classroom environment. She states, "When you're really connected to your students, you can deepen your instruction in ways that you can't when they don't feel safe with you. If they're not sure that you have a plan, that you have a sense of where you want to go in your lesson that day, even if you don't get there, then they feel unsafe. So I try to always start by framing the learning: 'Here's what I'd like to achieve today, and here's why it matters, and here's how the next forty-five minutes are going to break down. Are you ready to roll? Are you with me?' And off we go."

Jen describes the importance of being a prepared teacher. It's not only about preparing your content knowledge as a teacher. It's about laying the groundwork, the roadmap. Students will trust a teacher who has demonstrated organization and solid lesson planning. They will "roll" with the teacher when she decides to deviate from the lesson plan. In this way, organization begets agency.

Mariale Hardiman states that, "Neuroscientific evidence suggests that, if [students] do not recognize that the teacher's actions are goal-directed, the students will not simulate or internalize the teacher's thoughts and actions."[21] This is why it is important for teachers to use the board to share a syllabus, to write the agenda for the class period, to clarify steps toward completing homework assignments. Otherwise, students will maintain a hazy notion of what the teacher expects from them and distancing will take place.

English teacher Rob Crawford just returned to the classroom after a decade in full-time administration. Rob currently teaches at The Roxbury Latin School in West Roxbury, Massachusetts. Rob and I go back two decades to 1994, when we shared the same classroom. As young teachers, Rob and I found

21 Hardiman, Mariale M. (2003), *Connecting Brain Research with Effective Teaching* (New York: Rowman & Littlefield Education), p.151

immediate connection in our shared appreciation for the relational elements of teaching. Whether motivating our students to write – and express themselves – in their own poetry, or taking them on trips around the American West, Rob and I both appreciated the spirits within our students. It certainly was meaningful for me to see Rob back in his most genuine element, the classroom. A stoic, towering figure at the head of the classroom, Rob conveys the constant hum of warmth as he poses challenging questions while maintaining high expectations.

Rob states, "I would say one of the most important things that my time away from the classroom taught me is the importance of consistency and predictability. You build trust with students by letting them know exactly what the expectations of the course are going to be, what's expected of them every day, how they'll be evaluated, how everything will be weighted in the end in terms of their grade, and let them know exactly where they stand at all times. This is because kids know what to expect from you. There are no surprises. They know that you're not going to pull the rug out from under them.

> Neuroscientific evidence suggests that, if [students] do not recognize that the teacher's actions are goal-directed, the students will not simulate or internalize the teacher's thoughts and actions.

They know that you're not trying to trick them. They know that you're not setting up an obstacle course for them and whoever survives the obstacle course best wins. They know, *if I put forth this level of effort in this direction, in these ways, I can get an A in this class.*"

Like most teenagers today, the high school boys in Rob's care are extremely busy. The school he works at is an independent school based outside of Boston with a reputation for producing students well-prepared for college and beyond over the past 350 years. Therefore, the students have busy lives both inside and outside of school. Additionally, like all middle and high school students, these boys are growing into themselves. Their inner lives, their online lives, their school lives, and their home lives are constantly monitored. The idea of eliminating surprise assignments and sticking to the topic at hand supports this fact by ensuring that they will not need to worry about the outside variable of surprise.

"There's an unspoken code of honor that I think a teacher needs to have with his students which is, *I'm going to be 100% prepared because I'm asking you to be 100% prepared.* I think one of the reasons that I've built up a lot of trust with my students is they come to class knowing that I'm ready to go. I need to be on my toes. We know exactly what's going to happen in every class. There's going to be a quick little check on the reading. It's going to be appropriately challenging; we're going to have a discussion or we're going to play *Odyssey* Jeopardy. There's never really a surprise."

Rob also addresses the effect of "winging it" on his students. "I try to be an expert as much as I possibly can be on the topic because these kids know if you're winging it. They know if you aren't prepared. Another level of consistency where I build trust is, *Look. You're working hard, I'm working hard. You come ready to learn, I come ready to teach.* We kind of have this unspoken agreement. If I wing it even once a month, in a way that gives them the right to wing it too, even though as students they have no power and they actually can't wing it. It will affect their grade if they wing it."

> You can be the nicest person in the world, but if students are like, 'I don't know what we're doing in class,' that doesn't help even the nicest teacher

Winging it, or slacking on responsibility, sets the classroom up for tension between teachers and students. Rob articulates this through the lens of fairness. This "unspoken agreement" is a character-based contract supporting the notion that the classroom is a microcosm of equality. It acknowledges that both sides work hard, and implies that when that happens, an optimal learning environment results.

The Reverend Andrew Barnett, the Associate for Music and Worship at Cathedral School for Boys in Washington, D.C., offers a fantastic example of how important organization is toward being an effective teacher. He states, "You can be the nicest person in the world, but if students are like, 'I don't know what we're doing in class,' that doesn't help even the nicest teacher. Here's a story. I had some friends enrolled in nursing school at Yale. It was their first day of class. The bespectacled veteran of the nursing program asks, 'What describes good nurses?' Immediately, answers from the first-year nursing students flooded out, 'They're kind, sweet, nice, they love you…' The veteran teacher furrows her brow and tips spectacles on her nose and replies, 'Right. A nurse can do all those things. And also kill you.' Because if you don't have your stuff together, you cannot be a nurse. You can be the nicest, warmest person in the world, but if you don't have the organization to achieve, you could literally kill your patient." While a teacher would not physically kill his students, he absolutely could kill off ambition that takes so much time to generate by appearing blasé, flippant, and altogether unorganized.

Time to Get Comfortable

The word *comfort* is not one generally tossed around by schools. It conveys an image of lounging…on a hammock on the beach. Comfort is relaxation. However, it also is alleviation of pain or distress – a definition that resonates when exploring the school environment. If we were to honestly assess how our students are doing at the high school level, we would find that they are experiencing elevated stress levels, heightened anxiety, self-doubt, and feelings of being overwhelmed. These negative feelings are hopefully balanced by senses of possibility, exploration, community, and friendship. The inner lives of teenagers are rich with hope yet fraught with confusion. Therefore, when teachers focus on comfort, they show respect for the experience their students are undertaking.

Throughout our interview, Rob Crawford shared how he considers the student experience. "Kids have choices to make every night at home with their homework. With their electronic devices, with TV, with sleep, with whether to watch Game 7 of the World Series, or Monday Night Football, or a cool documentary on Basquiat. If you as a teacher want to do your students a favor, make it very clear what's expected of them the next day so that they don't have that worry and then that angst about, *What do I do tonight?*

"If every class made it very clear, *Here's what you have to do and here's how you'll be evaluated on it*, kids would have a much greater sense of comfort. They would know what they have to do and they would come to school prepared, ready to learn, and more likely to succeed in general. I've found, I think, in my earlier career when I didn't make expectations as clear every day, the really strong kids got A's no matter what. They did their reading whether it was checked or not. They were always prepared; they always went above and beyond. It's the middle kids and the kids who are less inclined to succeed in school who really, really benefit from clear expectations and follow-through by the teacher on exactly what he or she said they were going to do."

I appreciate Rob's use of the word "comfort" here. I hadn't heard it used before regarding the teacher's responsibility in the classroom, but it sums it up so well because that word connotes a weight, like a gravitas. But it also implies a softness. The more I mulled over his use of that word, the more I realized that it's the exact definition of what a student would want her classroom to be because to be in a comfortable environment means, "Okay.

My anxiety levels are down because I'm not worried or resentful, or worried about the fact that I did the work but my neighbor didn't."

In his use of the term "comfort," Rob also touches on the importance of fairness. Kids really look at fairness in the context of work ethic and how fairness begets trust. By knowing that the teacher is not going to surprise them or deviate from the syllabus, students enter class prepared and ready for what they know lies ahead. In Rob's classroom, they know that each class begins with a three-question reading quiz. The quiz is fact-based and designed to build confidence because if they did their nightly reading, they will score perfectly. There also is consistency in the type of question asked on the daily quiz.

"The students come in feeling not only comfortable, but they come in and they're just talking with each other, and I say, 'Okay guys, sit down and get ready.' They sit there like, 'Bring it on. Here it comes.' They're not worried at all." Rob has mastered a method of achieving comfort without coddling and without losing the mission of the optimal classroom as an ongoing learning environment.

Time to Let Students Trust You

When trust is established, a class can soar to amazing heights. Trust is central toward forging close connections, but it takes time to build. Jordan, a student from California, puts it this way, "I think definitely it's about trust and how that opens so many doors for learning. Once you feel safe and once you're encouraged, then you want to open up. Once you open up, you feel great about it. I think for me, once those things happen, I start to thrive in that subject. I start to feel a real connection with that teacher. I imagine that's definitely a big part about teaching because you're trying get someone to understand, and they have to understand you first before they try to push you even further."

Trust is based on stability. Learning is diminished when a teacher is unpredictable. Unpredictable authority figures at work or at home put us all on edge. Stable homes generate predictable behaviors from parent to child. Basic needs are met, and the child grows with a strong locus of control.

Enrique Martínez Celaya, a world-renowned painter and sculptor, notes, "I believe that kids read adults better than adults – they recognize trust and follow if the right one. Adults can't see clearly because they've camouflaged themselves/identities in words." As we grow into adults, we develop a fluency with words that obfuscate and elaborate. When used in the former manner, students are put off, as they sense a disconnect between a teacher's actions and words. However, when used in the latter manner, their teacher's words can benefit the student by broadening a lesson through elaboration.

Brazilian educator Paulo Freire notes how easily trust can break when a teacher allows the "do as I say, not as I do" maxim to exist in his classroom. Freire writes, "Trust is established by dialogue. False love, false humility, and feeble faith in others cannot create trust. Trust is contingent on the evidence which one party provides the other of his true, concrete intentions; it cannot exist if that party's words do not coincide with their actions. To say one thing and do another – to take one's own words lightly – cannot inspire trust. To glorify democracy and to silence the people is a farce; to discourse on humanism and to negate people is a lie."[22]

> Trust is contingent on the evidence which one party provides the other of his true, concrete intentions; it cannot exist if that party's words do not coincide with their actions.

Colleen Kyle

History teacher Colleen Kyle speaks of how she builds trust through confident command of course content, which frees her to explore the thought

22 Freire, Paulo (1968), *Pedagogy of the Oppressed* (New York: Penguin Education), p.72

processes of students in her classroom. "I think students want to trust you. They generally assume that you have the knowledge. I've looked at a lot of different faculty evaluations at this point, and even for a teacher who's struggling to connect with students, they usually trust the teacher expertise." Teacher expertise – in curriculum and instruction – is something students recognize at the base level. Once that confidence is established, the teacher can develop areas of connection through trust-building. Moments like critical feedback and assessments provide opportunities for trust to be generated or broken. These are profoundly sensitive aspects of teaching which impact the student-teacher dynamic.

Colleen continues, "Even if you're teaching something new that you haven't taught before and your grasp may feel more shallow than your grasp of other subjects you've taught for a long time, the students tend to trust that you know what you're doing. What you have to prove next is to make your material important to the student. You need to make it personally relevant. You need to let them know that you see them and you hear them, and I would say that I have some colleagues that inspired me lately to be more overt in saying, 'I hear you. I see you. I trust you.'"

English teacher Jen Dohr concurs and shares a parallel example about a colleague who physically ensured that every student was feeling heard, seen, and trusted. "This teacher would knock on each desk as she would say, 'I *see* you,' and it was so powerful. I remember the first time I saw her do that and was deeply moved. It was this combination of this physical closeness and this 'in your face' you matter to me so much, I'm not going to let you hide. It's what I mean when I suggest that a teacher is deepening when she is connecting, because once you connect then you're 'in their face' enough to deepen. Then the more you deepen, the more they know you care. Teaching becomes this loop of ever-deepening compassion and care."

Learning is an incredibly nuanced, emotional, and challenging activity. The nuance in learning comes with calibrating how best to retain the material. The emotion in learning comes with finding a "hook" to unhitch feelings of connection to the material as well as relating to the teacher, generating feelings of competency. The challenge of learning comes with adapting to a previously unknown concept, theory, or mindset that builds neuroconnectivity as a result. Teaching is the same, but for different reasons. Teaching involves nuance, which comes into play when differentiating instruction, communicating feedback, and managing pace. Teaching also involves emotion because an expert teacher is constantly gauging the emotional barometer of the room to ensure the students are following their line of thought. Teaching involves challenge because concepts can be complex, and excellent teaching requires hard work toward making inroads in successfully teaching those concepts. Overarching both teaching and learning is the central notion of trust. Trust is the connection point between students and teachers.

Roxbury Latin School English teacher Rob Crawford sums up the importance of trust in both teaching and learning, "It all comes down to, 'What are we trying to do here?' What we're trying to do is we're trying to teach. The goal is learning."

> What we're trying to do is we're trying to teach. The goal is learning.

I have always believed that when you're excited about hiring a teacher, you've ideally found somebody who is of that frame of mind. A candidate may have a Ph.D. and present herself as the expert in her field, but if she's not an expert learner herself, she will encounter challenges in the classroom.

Rob continues, "Teaching is about the learning. It's not about being the expert. Through teaching, I am able to continue learning about myself. For example, I'm the expert in teaching, I'm not the expert on *The Odyssey*. I'm an expert on 14 and 15-year- old boys learning 24 hours a day." And he honors it. "I bring a perspective of realizing what a privilege it is to have the opportunity to be a teacher."

Time to Grapple

In the book, *The Students Are Watching*, Ted and Nancy Sizer write, "Most teachers are fond of the word, 'engagement,' because it means that the students are really taking an interest in the work which the teacher has designed for them. Grappling, however, goes one step further. It presumes that the student has something to add to the story. Either hypothetically or actually, the student is asked to join the struggle, to add his or her input."[23] Generous competition is based on students grappling with concepts; many times, they are grappling with the teacher as well.

Over breakfast at a Harvard Square café, Nancy elaborated, saying, "Grappling students are not focused on pleasing the teacher, and that's as it should be. They want to talk and ask questions and disagree with each other. If we are afraid to give them the time and space to grapple because it feels uncomfortable, these otherwise engaged students tune out. They need time to practice this essential skill, as it is based in precise questioning and mutual respect."

---

23 Sizer, Nancy and Sizer, Ted (1999), *The Students are Watching* (Boston: Beacon Press), p.25

The teacher posits a theory and the students go at it, at times disagreeing with the teacher. This can be uncomfortable for the teacher, as it can threaten the power dynamic. An insecure teacher might falter when his theory is challenged. Yet the relational teacher takes time to truly listen to students as he is being challenged, for when students feel they are sincerely, honestly, and seriously heard, they build closer bridges. The more opportunities students have to grapple with their teacher and classmates, the sharper their critical thinking skills become.

> (Student) resistance turned out not to be resistance at all but some life-problem that I had just misread.

In his book, *The Heart of Teaching*, educator Stephen Wangh explains how we tend to personalize student disagreement as defiance when, in actuality, for him, "(Student) resistance turned out not to be resistance at all but some life-problem that I had just misread."[24] Wangh considers every time a student challenges a teacher to be a test of the teacher's belief in the student. "To pass the 'test,' a teacher may need real patience, for the student wants to sense that the teacher will 'be there' for the student, even when the student is difficult."[25] Ted and Nancy Sizer take a different approach to the same argument by explaining the detriment of a teacher who avoids disagreement in the classroom. "To treat adolescents as delicate flowers unable to act and think is a costly pretense, as patronizing as it is wasteful."[26] These words are prescient, as today we struggle with the "snowflake generation," which is stereotyped as weak in spirit and quick to crumble in the face of adversity and discomfort.

The teacher-student relationship is not a one-way street in which the teacher imparts information to the learner. When grappling occurs, it's a result of dialogue that has become intensified – almost as if the words from both sides are rubbing against each other in a scrum to determine which side wins, knowing that ultimately both sides will emerge the winner.

Time to Validate

"If I sense that my teacher believes in me, I will work incredibly hard for that teacher." That message was resoundingly clear when meeting with students from all over the U.S. However, in my teacher interviews, another message

---

24 Wangh, Stephen (2013), *The Heart of Teaching* (New York: Routledge Press), p.63
25 Ibid.
26 Sizer, Nancy and Sizer, Ted (1999), *The Students are Watching* (Boston: Beacon Press), p.24

was implied: "If my student believes in me, my work will go farther." Trust is a two-way connection. It matters to a student to feel known and believed in by a teacher, and it matters just as much that a teacher feels believed in by students.

The caliber of a lesson sinks dramatically in classrooms that brazenly disrespect the teacher. Over time, broken trust and broken respect lie at the core of most ineffective learning. Teachers need time to build and maintain trust – particularly since trust can be broken easily, and is nearly impossible to regain.

English teacher Rob Crawford feels that an easy way to break trust with students is to be perceived as favoring a student. "I would never tell a student, 'That was brilliant,' even if it was brilliant because suddenly there's jealousy for that student among his classmates. To say that brilliant comment, he put in the exact same amount of effort as another boy who made maybe an average comment.

"All the boys know who the geniuses are in the class. They've been with these kids since 6th grade. There are certain boys who get A+'s in every class. They truly are intellectually gifted. I want the kids who struggle to get B–'s and C+'s to feel just as intellectual and just as valued as those kids who literally can put in slightly less effort and still get an A.

"For me to say, 'Brilliant comment,' to anyone, I now have to be very aware. Now I have to keep track because if I say it to one kid, I actually need to find a way to say it to every kid sometime in the next week. What I'll say if a kid makes a brilliant comment, which isn't rare, it happens all the time, is I'll say, 'That's fascinating. I didn't think of that.'"

In Stanford University Professor Carol Dweck's *Mindset*, she advises parents and teachers to avoid making comments about a person's innate qualities. To say, "you're brilliant" is to imply that a student's brilliance is an innate quality. Saying, "that's fascinating" puts the focus on the comment, as opposed to the commentator. It also allows for deeper analysis of the "fascinating" comment. When something is referred to as "brilliant," it connotes perfection, which cannot be further broadened or critiqued.

In a recent NPR (National Public Radio) article titled, "Why Teachers Need to Know the Wrong Answers," Harvard University science professor Philip Sadler states, "Teachers who find their kids' ideas fascinating are just better teachers than teachers who find the subject matter fascinating."[27] Among teachers with a deep relational understanding of their students, there is greater success than among teachers who do not know their students.

---

27 http://www.npr.org/sections/ed/2016/04/16/473273571/why-teachers-need-to-know-the-wrong-answers

A successful teacher brings wide-eyed curiosity not merely to the subject matter, but also to how their individual students think and learn. The same NPR article asserts that "Research has demonstrated that among teachers with stronger knowledge of student weaknesses, their students learned significantly more science, based on a retest at the end of the year."[28] Teachers need time to understand and to be fascinated by their students' learning strengths and weaknesses.

Teachers who find their kids' ideas fascinating are just better teachers than teachers who find the subject matter fascinating.

Rob continues, "It's all about effort, it's all about valuing everyone's comments. I'd say another very powerful thing that builds trust is I almost never share my opinion. I almost never ask questions where there is a right or wrong answer. I tell my students that even though it takes a lot of restraint, I'm not going to share with them what I think. 'I think everything that you guys said has validity and I really appreciate you contributing that.' I think if they were to make fun of me they would say, 'Mr. C. says all the time there is no right or wrong answer.'"

English teacher Jen Dohr views teacher feedback in class discussions as a powerful means to communicate care. This care, when received openly, strengthens trust between student and teacher. "Sometimes in the classroom it's almost like the student is coming in with a statement and then as the teacher you are trying to qualify it with the character or storyline or theme being discussed. It's a drive to connect to what she's said." This "drive to connect" involves an impressive amount of optimism and flexibility. The optimism lies in the unconditional belief that the student's comment is earnest, not flippant or half-baked. Because it is deemed earnest, it is worthy of validation. So what Jen describes here is the act of validating a student contribution with an open mind. The student recognizes this on a deep level and trust develops between both.

"I think that's how connection happens because the student (and the classmates witnessing this event) is receiving the message from you, she cares about what I think. I don't think that there exists any more powerful message you can send to a student. Sometimes it has to be explicitly said: Here's the ball. Catch it, toss it around with each other. I already know what I think, I'm boring myself. I've read this book so many times, I don't want to just hear myself talk. I'm feeling kind of lonely up here! Why would I care what Spark

28 Ibid.

Notes thinks? Perhaps we should make a lesson out of all their errors. I think you guys can do better than they do...

"The key is you have to mean it, and I do mean it. I think kids blow away Spark Notes. And when students regularly get the message, 'my teacher cares what I think,' then those same kids will end up coming to see you with a, 'hey, can I talk to you about my dad, he's really ill', or 'hey, I just couldn't focus today, I've got this thing going on with this girl.'"

Jen recognizes that what she is doing is building trust through genuine validation. The student now thinks, "you know, if she cares this much about what I think about *To Kill a Mockingbird,* she must care what I think about everything." With this trust established, the learning is limitless and the potential to make a deep impact on content and student character is massive. It really is all about building trust – and not breaking it.

In the words of Landon, an 11-year-old, "I think that if you really have true trust in a teacher, you're not going to lose it ever. You really can hold it, because trust is something they don't give you on a test or by playing favorites. A good teacher would never do such a thing, and I feel like you can have a true trust in someone who would never risk losing it by doing something like that."

Recapping the Relational: Teaching Trust

Trust takes a long time to build and it can be broken in a nanosecond. As teachers, we keep this in the forefront of our minds every day while in the classroom. Students look to us not only to instruct but to provide mentoring on how to live. That is a lot to ask! We are human, thus fallible. Yet we are charged with the heavy responsibility to be our best selves every moment while at school. This stuff matters because the students are watching.

In order to present trust, we must receive trust when deserved. Teachers in Finland come from a highly selective two-year master's program in education before being given their classroom. They hold unconditional trust from the first day of school. This trust is earned and they feel respected. The feeling of respect results from being given autonomy to create curriculum and deliver instruction as they best see fit for their class. They work in trusting collaboration with their colleagues.

But again, it is worth repeating that trust is earned. A teacher does not begin the school year with automatic trust from the students. They might be polite and dutiful during the first weeks of school, but the students are not trusting. Trust occurs when teachers follow through with their commitments to the students. Papers are handed back on time and the lesson plan is concretely laid out. Teachers might start each class the same way every day

Rob Crawford

– such as Rob Crawford's three-question quiz at the beginning of each class. Students expect it; the teacher delivers.

There is no favoritism, no "that's brilliant!", no humiliation of students, no matter how tired and overloaded the teacher feels. There is attention paid to the value of student contributions, even if they are different than what the teacher predicts. There is comfort in routine. There is safety felt when a teacher communicates, "I see you. I hear you. I trust you." Trust is the foundation in a classroom where grappling is taking place. When a teacher trusts that the belligerent student is not being disrespectful but rather trying out a new idea for the first time. Most of all, trust is caring. When students know in the bottom of their souls that their teacher cares about what they think, say, and do . . . that, to me, is the heart of relational teaching.

Jamie Neilson

Time to reflect

"I am a writer of books in retrospect.
I talk in order to understand;
I teach in order to learn."

Robert Frost

It's one thing to possess passion for a subject. It's another to take that seed of passion and enable it to grow into a flourishing curriculum. It can often feel like teachers need to be careful about dipping their toes into the rushing current; they risk getting sucked into the Class V rapids of modern-day school expectations. Yet they don't have a choice. Teachers are expected to do so much, above and beyond classroom teaching. Every teacher I spoke with shared a desire for the pace of the day, week, month, and year to slow down and allow for "time to just stop – and shake off the unnecessary stuff and lock in the important stuff."

"You're so lucky to have the entire summer off. And all the holidays during the school year. And Spring Break!" How often we've heard these comments from people who don't teach! More often than not, however, teachers spend the time that they have off catching up on work they've been unable to take care of during the year. They learn new technologies, familiarize themselves with emerging educational issues and practical solutions, and attend professional seminars, retreats, and conferences.

In addition, teachers don't forget about students during vacation time.

Instead, they often gain clarity about issues that seemed insurmountable during the school year. The deepest teaching issues – those that cannot be resolved quickly and require sustained, reflective thought – can only be worked out by teachers on their own time and at their own pace. Solutions might emerge after reading a book or newspaper article a teacher discovers because she finally has time to read, or during a serendipitous conversation with a friend over brunch.

The deepest teaching issues – those that cannot be resolved quickly and require sustained, reflective thought – can only be worked out by teachers on their own time and at their own pace.

We are starving for reflection time. We exist in a 24/7 environment defined by personal technology. There is no reason to be unreachable when you carry a smartphone, or to be bored when you have wireless streaming.

What does this mean for our students? Without reflection time, we are unable to fully retain information. We are losing the necessary time required to apply acquired information to current classroom themes. Schools can help prevent this emotional starvation by becoming havens for reflective thinking – largely without technology.

Again, Finland appears to be quite rational in terms of delineating the appropriate level of technology integration into schools. Fourth Grade teacher Meghan Elizabeth says, "Finnish schools utilize much lower technology than in the United States, I would say. We are very low-tech. We have projectors. We have some whiteboards in every other classroom, so every other year a kid will have a Smart Board in their class. Chalkboards are still there."

The irony here is that as a country, Finland is very high-tech. "Finland is the place where you can buy something from the vending machine with your phone. You can buy a public transport ticket with your phone. You can do all kinds of things with your phone like pay for your bike. Kids have phones starting when they start school. Yet Finnish schools are very low-tech and a lot more traditional, with a focus on interacting with other people."

A *New York Times* article by Matt Richtel discusses Silicon Valley executives who are sending their children to technology-free Waldorf schools in California's Upper Peninsula. "While other schools in the region brag about their wired classrooms, the Waldorf school embraces a simple, retro look — blackboards with colorful chalk, bookshelves with encyclopedias, wooden desks filled with workbooks and No. 2 pencils." Paul Thomas, a former teacher and an associate professor of education at Furman University interviewed for the article, states, "Teaching is a human experience," adding, "Technology is a distraction when we need literacy, numeracy and critical thinking." The article concludes with an insight from Pierre Laurent, a Silicon Valley executive, "Engagement is about human contact, the contact with the teacher, the contact with their peers."[29]

I've spent a lot of time over the past year writing this book in cafes, airports, and libraries in and around London. I have been struck by parents accompanied by a child or toddler who set themselves up at a table and pick up their smartphones before even retrieving their coffees. The child in the stroller, or the toddler sitting in the booster seat, is typically left to his own devices. It doesn't take long for the child, who is not receiving any attention from his parents, to cause a bit of a disruption.

> Kids have phones starting when they start school. Yet Finnish schools are very low-tech and a lot more traditional, with a focus on interacting with other people.

Imagine being that child. The neurons in his brain are fusing, growing, and multiplying at a dizzying rate. His sensory skills are in overdrive. He notices shimmering light and a wide range of colors that present themselves to him like a prism. Sounds flood his ear canals. He wants to share all of this with his parents, so he looks up. Yet instead of looking into their eyes, he sees furrowed brow-lines above a rectangular object that has no response. So he starts pressing his face against the wall, licking the table, or eating his fingers with eyes heartbreakingly absent of light.

There is a generation of such children growing up today. I call them Generation Compete. They are competing with machines for human connection. As these cute babies and toddlers develop into not-so-cute teens years from now, we do not know how this will manifest itself. But we will know soon enough – far too late to rectify.

The concept of boredom is a diminishing commodity. When we are bored, we are not "doing nothing." Rather, we are allowing our brains time to work through information. Like during REM sleep, time spent daydreaming is time spent making sense of the stimuli that life presents us. In his thoughtful book,

---

29 http://www.nytimes.com/2011/10/23/technology/at-waldorf-school-in-silicon-valley-technology-can-wait.html?mcubz=0

The End of Absence, Michael Harris notes that, "As we embrace a technology's gifts, we usually fail to consider what they ask from us in return—the subtle, hardly noticeable payments we make in exchange for their marvelous service. We don't notice, for example, that the gaps in our schedules have disappeared because we're too busy delighting in the amusements that fill them. We forget the games that childhood boredom forged because boredom itself has been outlawed. Why would we bother to register the end of solitude, of ignorance, of lack? Why would we care that an absence has disappeared?"[30]

From an educator's point of view, my answer would be that we should care a lot. Students need reflection time to make sense of the information shared in their myriad classes. Ted and Nancy Sizer explain that, "Much of a young person's work that counts academically takes place in private time – the minutes or hours during which puzzlement can become understanding."[31] I love the expression "puzzlement can become understanding." It's like a "just add water" approach to learning, in which time is the water. Understanding is the planted seed.

> Much of a young person's work that counts academically takes place in private time – the minutes or hours during which puzzlement can become understanding.

Teachers need reflection time to create lesson plans containing incentives thoughtfully crafted from deep knowledge of students. Schools need reflection time to ensure that they continue to operate in line with their mission.

The end of absence, the end of boredom, the end of imaginary time, also risks the end of time for empathy. Reflection time gives us the opportunity to address and dissect situations that occurred during the school day. From a student's perspective, it's, "Did I insult my classmate when I made my argument?" From a teacher's perspective, it's, "Did I intend to respond so quickly to that student's class contribution?" Harris states, "One doesn't see teenagers staring into space anymore. Gone is the idle mind of the adolescent."[32] But aren't idle hands the devil's playground? Not when it pertains to learning and growing as ethical, moral young adults.

30 Harris, Michael (2015), *The End of Absence* (New York: Penguin Books), p.14
31 Sizer, Nancy and Sizer, Ted (1999), *The Students Are Watching* (Boston: Beacon Press), p.54
32 Harris, Michael (2015), *The End of Absence* (New York: Penguin Books), p.47

Time to Have a Chat

I learned about the importance of reflection time long before becoming a teacher, when I was 12 years old at Camp Becket in Massachusetts. Becket was an incredible experience for me; even at that young age, I knew that in nine weeks I was growing in more ways than during the nine months of school. The tradition that taught me about the importance of reflection time was called "Cabin Chat." Every night, after preparing for sleep, the two counselors and eight campers would congregate around a candle in the center of the cabin floor. The bunks were situated so that everyone could face the candle. The two counselors sat in the middle of the room, next to the candle, yet somehow it felt as if we were all part of a circle of ten.

One of the counselors would begin cabin chat with a "highlight or lowlight of the day." We'd share one of either in the darkness, knowing that everyone was hearing us even though we couldn't see anyone. The other counselor would then ask the "question of the night." The question would be open-ended – an "essential question" that had no right or wrong answer. The cabin contract we'd designed on the first night of camp stipulated that there would be no judgment when sharing our answers to these sometimes personal, always revealing questions. We were safe. Trust built each day through our shared experiences, and at night through our vulnerable authenticity.

Cabin chat was the overnight camp equivalent of the large oval Harkness Table. It was an opportunity for us to express our hopes and fears, beliefs and doubts. As a counselor, I responded to some heady personal revelations. Parents divorcing. Sibling illnesses. Developing identities and values. Cabin chat risked breaking down into tears or erupting into laughter.

Cabin chat was a scheduled time for reflection that came at the end of a busy day. Campers counted on it, as it was non-negotiable. In my five years as a Becket counselor, I didn't hear a single objection to cabin chat. Yet I did receive several requests for cabin chat on overnight camping trips – followed by relief when I said that cabin chat was essential for every night, regardless of where we are.

Even at nine years old, campers recognized the importance of reflection. The candlelight reflected flames of ideas and emotions while the campers opened up. They took inventory of themselves during the highlight or lowlight they chose to present. The follow-up questions were thoughtful, and only asked when the camper's contribution was vague or particularly in need of unpacking. Everyone was extremely focused, although sometimes a particularly fatigued camper would succumb to sleep.

I learned a lot about teaching during my years as a camp counselor. How to foster strong group dynamics. The importance of accepting others. The need to connect through stories that exposed our strengths and areas of challenge. The importance of being known – for our achievements and for our individual traits, beliefs, and backgrounds. Cabin chat sums this up as a visual, concrete example of the coaching side of teaching.

Jeff Domina, an English teacher at independent boarding school Phillips Academy in Andover, Massachusetts, was a camp counselor with me. He speaks about what he applies to his classroom from his experiences at Camp Becket. "I've been looking for something like cabin chat, which is really special. Opportunities to model openness, vulnerability and comfort with complexity, unanswerability and constructive tension and confusion. The kind of ambiguity that makes your mind hold more than one idea at the same time, not the unclear fuzzy kind of ambiguity. I thought that was valuable in cabin chat and it remains incredibly valuable in classroom discussion as well."

> The soufflé will not rise unless there is time allotted to reflect and ask the essential teacher question: "Are you with me so far?

Without reflection time, this ambiguity is a scramble in shambles because it has no structure. Without time to reflect on the idea being explored, students cannot make room for "complexity, unanswerability, and constructive tension." Yet it is precisely this ambiguity that serves as the core of sponge-squeezing, water-generating thinking in the classroom. Jeff describes these moments with clear awareness of their value in the class experience and the learning process. Time must slow down when the lesson veers toward complexity. Time must be carved to decelerate classroom momentum so that ideas can be molded. These ideas can bake in complexity piece by piece, yet the soufflé will not rise unless there is time allotted to reflect and ask the essential teacher question: "Are you with me so far?"

Time to Find Power in the Pause

Receiving an assignment on the heels of a deep-level discussion can provide students with an opportunity to reflect. For a class conversation to involve deep-level dialogue, students need to feel comfortable with the natural ebb and flow of conversation. The classroom environment should be relaxed and a level of trust previously established. Risk-taking is embraced, as long as it is earnest and furthers the conversation.

Being able to think critically while holding more than one idea at the same time can only come with time for reflection. In order for a teacher to keep up with the comments and commentators, he needs to have time to reflect. This reflection time can come in the form of a break in discussion, when he can offer a summary of the discourse (or, perhaps better, delegate a student to do this). Alternatively, it can come with a group work assignment, which affords the teacher time to assess the conversation while students are occupied with the assignment.

Jen Dohr, the English teacher at The Archer School in Los Angeles, expresses how it feels for a teacher to keep track of the different layers of conversation that exist during reflective class discussion. "You feel it when you've lost them. They're not going to take risks, they're not going to trust you. You can't be authentic unless you're connecting. The moment you lose that connection is the moment when there are just words coming out of your mouth, and you're no longer aware of where they are. You're just talking. It can happen to a first-year teacher, and it can happen to a twenty-three-year veteran, like me. You are never above it… I think the less experienced teacher will just keep rolling with the lesson plan, thinking 'I'll find my way back if I stick with the content.'

"The truth is, you won't ever find your way back through content. You'll only find your way back by stopping, taking a deep breath, looking at them in the eye, getting a little closer to them, maybe knocking on each desk, and asking them, 'Wait, where are you? Let's back up for a minute. I think I may have lost you. That question may have been a little too tough. Tell me where you are now'. If you don't reconnect with them as individuals, if you keep riding with content, you've lost them. You can feel it in the room. They are looking down, they're fidgeting, they're turning to each other, and you've lost them.

"The great thing is that you can get them back if you stop. You have to have the confidence to pause because it's hard in the moment. You think, 'I'll just shove a little more content at them, and then they'll trust me, and then I'll be back in my saddle, and off we'll ride.' No, you'll be off your saddle. You'll be flat on the floor!"

The irony in Jen's description is that you won't make forward strides unless you first stop to reflect. The temptation to steamroll, to continue forging ahead despite the pit-in-your-stomach knowledge that you have derailed the train, is a natural one. We tend to think, if we move ahead, we can reconnect the wheels to the rails. Jen articulately details the inner thoughts of the teacher, and in them it is clear that the teacher recognizes that there is a disconnect happening. Yet the drive to push forward, especially in this age of standardized test requirements and other factors creating pressure to "push through the curriculum," is completely understandable.

There is power in the pause. This power will get you back in the saddle, as opposed to sitting on the floor, having just been bucked off the horse. The power in the pause comes from a place of confidence, not weakness. We tend to view taking a step back as a sign of weakness, the result of a mistake. In the classroom, nothing is further from the truth. The worst that can happen is that the teacher has misread the climate of the class. Maybe, through taking a pause, she'll even discover that the students were following her all along.

> We tend to view taking a step back as a sign of weakness, the result of a mistake. In the classroom, nothing is further from the truth.

Time to Find Islands in the River

When reflection time results in a realization that alterations need to be made to a lesson, a relational teacher uses their agency to tweak the lesson. The entire class will benefit. However, this can only happen if a teacher is given time to reflect on the pace, focus, delivery, and completion of the lesson. Perhaps with renewed focus on integrating time to reflect in schools, we could raise a generation that incorporates this practice into their lives, with everyone benefitting as a result.

What would need to happen to create the perfect school schedule that includes time to reflect?

Alan Rivera, the world language teacher from The Park School in Brookline, Massachusetts, states, "I think part of a really wonderful schedule includes islands in the river that give teachers time to observe and to reflect, and to create something, and to figure out how to implement it. All those things are things that you can't do in a school day or you can't do in a free period. You can't go watch another teacher teach in a period. You can't think about, 'What was good about that?' You can't figure out, 'How do I want to adapt what I'm doing in the classroom with what I just saw in a period?' You can't then figure out a lesson in a period. It takes a lot of time. But it is time well spent because giving teachers time to exit their own classroom and to explore a colleague's classroom and to bring certain elements back to their own classroom is hugely important."

To me, what Alan describes is analogous to planning a field trip. You explain to students why you've planned the trip and prepare them for the trip, take the trip, and then reflect on the experience with the entire class after it is over. You draw connections between what you saw and the curricular theme of the course.

Applying the idea of reflection to professionalism, observing other teachers enables the observer to see new approaches to teaching, interacting with students, and creating optimal classroom models. However, after a 45-minute period of observing a colleague, teachers need time to be able to bake ideas into their own approach to teaching. As we know, with all the class periods in a day and all the other responsibilities teachers shoulder, it seems like 90% of what you see during third period is forgotten by seventh period.

If you're going to have a school that comprises lifelong learners, it should support the humility that says, "I know that I don't know everything." The school can then be an incubator where teachers are encouraged to use best practices and to learn from each other and improve together. If schools can design a schedule with that type of collaborative reflection time baked into it, they can produce huge rewards in both productivity and morale.

Alan concludes, "I think every single school is grappling with this issue. Sometimes I think it's only us, and then you go to other schools and you're talking to them then you realize every school is trying to figure this puzzle out. It's just not easy. It's very complex. I think that the answer lies in taking the time to sit together and talk as a community of teachers. If you figure something out that's better, you give it a try – with the support of your colleagues."

Imagine how amazing it would be to have a generation of students grow into adulthood after having had their schooling designed with time for reflection. Envision a school that considers the time that it takes for students to grow optimally; a school that factors reflection time, connection time, and time to learn from mistakes into its daily schedule.

Time to Go to the Chapel

Many parochial schools toss a stone into the river of the weekly schedule by including Chapel. Chapel time can take many forms, depending on the identity of the school. For example, at The Episcopal School in Los Angeles, California, Chapel takes place three times a week. Jamie Neilson, the Upper School Director, defines Chapel's importance in the following way, "We have found that the kids see the clergy here as being their touchstone. Our Head of School (a priest herself) is very clear about the pastoral role of the school." Led by the Rector, Chaplains, and/or Head of School, Chapel becomes a place and time for the entire school community to come together, take a temperature check, collaborate on a lesson, and meditate in contemplative reflection for a few guaranteed minutes of the busy school day.

Chapel is also an opportunity for students to plant themselves more snugly into the entire school community. Suzanne Buck, the Head of School and Rector at Chatham Hall School in Chatham, Virginia, says Chapel provides an opportunity for individual students to be known in a clear and unique way. "Chapel is a time for reflection and contemplation, and a time for students to openly share what's salient and meaningful for them." Much like in the classroom, Chapel is a time where teachers can reach the students fluidly. The idea of fluidity is so important for teachers, as the term identifies the essence of being attuned and nimble regarding where the kids are at during any given time.

"We begin each chapel service by asking two questions: '*Who* are you?' and '*Whose* are you?' Through our chapel program, we are creating reflective and contemplative time where some of us can be synthesized and come together."

Suzanne's thoughts helped me appreciate the idea of reflection time benefitting not just the individual but large groups as well. The image of reflection time that comes to my mind has always been the monk on the top of the mountain or Abraham going to the desert, involved in solitary reflection. But Suzanne broadens the idea of reflection time to be more of a time for community empowerment. Her questions, "Who are you?" and "Whose are you?" are both so beautifully articulated.

It's this idea to me, that whatever the being or the spirit is of *whose* you are, it's an image of outstretched arms around you – you're never alone. The idea of fluidity – not flexibility, but fluidity – is curious, because flexibility is discussed a lot. I love the idea of fluidity because of the liquid image it presents. The idea of not just flexibility but adaptability is a trait that liquids possess. There is a likeness here to the spirit in that the humanity that exists within a school is moldable and malleable much like water. When Suzanne addresses the importance of teachers recognizing the fluidity of their students, she is really addressing the identification of the malleable spirit each student possesses.

The image of water is also pertinent to the larger concept of schools. I have been involved with the building of several new schools, and I always compared it to the process of building canals in Venice. You can plan the canals, you can plan the blueprint of the city, and you can dig the canals with a strong degree of certainty regarding how the water will flow within them. But it's not until you actually add the water that you know that the canals are flowing the way they should. The same holds true with schools. We can build school walls in anticipation of how students will flow within those walls, but the added element – the unpredictable variable that comes with the human spirit – leaves room for surprise.

Witnessing and validating the human condition through Chapel is a precise example of the benefits of school-wide reflection time. It contributes to developing a sense of who one is at both the human and spiritual level. It does not need to be religiously oriented, either. It is about taking time in the day at least once a week and being one within the fabric of a community larger than oneself. As Jamie Neilson stated earlier in the chapter, "Time to Sidebar", we have thousands of moments where we "brush up" against each other during the school day, resulting in a calibration of our individual "ethical compass." Chapel – or assembly, or town hall, or whatever the name, – is a chance to recalibrate the collective ethical compass of the school, *together*.

> We can build school walls in anticipation of how students will flow within those walls, but the added element – the unpredictable variable that comes with the human spirit – leaves room for surprise.

Time to Circle Up

An article in *Responsive Classroom* by Dana Lynn Januszka and Kristen Vincent describes "closing circle" as an end-of-the-school-day ritual that Kristen uses every day in her fourth-grade classroom. Closing circle in the classroom serves a similar purpose to cabin chat in overnight camp. "Like morning meeting at the beginning of the day, closing circle brings a sense of calm, safety, and community to students and teachers," say Dana and Kristen. "The routine also helps students practice reflecting on what's meaningful to them about their schoolwork, their classmates, and themselves."[33]

Every adult and student in the classroom takes part in closing circle. The students are empty-handed and free from distraction as they face each other. Contributors focus on positive elements of the present or future, while sometimes reflecting on the past. They celebrate accomplishments, discuss skills to improve, and close with a chant, song, or cheer. The positive tone sends students off to carpool on a high. By being asked to reflect on the entire day, they can't help but feel a sense of wonder at all the concepts, activities, and experiences to which they were exposed. Consequently, the students' overall excitement about school rises, and the likelihood that they'll look forward to returning the next day increases.

Technology is notably absent from closing circle. You can't reflect when

33   https://www.responsiveclassroom.org/closing-circle/

you're in the middle of the public square. Reflection needs to happen without devices. Reflection is greater when uninterrupted: when the temptation to lose focus is reduced.

Neuroscientists have identified two systems of attention and associated thought. "One is directed outward," says Daniel Willingham for *The New York Times*, "as when you scroll through your e-mail or play Candy Crush. The other is directed inward, as when you daydream, plan what you'll do tomorrow, or reflect on the past."[34] Digital activities direct us outward, and since the two modes toggle with each other (when one is on, the other is off), spending lots of time with devices means we spend less time reflecting. Instead, we are switching lanes on the freeway, concentrating on the zigzag rather than our inner thoughts. Cabin chat, closing circle, and simple mindfulness moments throughout the school day are all about exercising the inward direction of thinking.

Teacher-led closing circles help to ensure that the tone is positive and supportive. Willingham addresses the shadow-side of reflection when he states, "Reflection can turn ugly, as when we ruminate about some past insult or error."[35] By being given time to reflect with his students, a teacher can prevent the negative fallout from overthinking about the negative. And a teacher can also allow time to value the daydreams, hopes, and goals that result from inward reflection in a supportive and positive classroom environment.

One teacher who went above and beyond all of this is Christopher ("Chris") Ulmer, who created a viral video about how he flips the closing circle tradition by beginning every school day with an opening circle tradition. The video spotlights Chris, the teacher of a wide-ranging group of elementary school students. Chris made a pledge to begin each school day by calling each student to his desk, shaking the student's hand, and telling the student one reason why he is a fantastic student. In turn, the student beams, visibly infused with vigor and confidence about the day ahead. The fact that more teachers aren't doing this is no reflection on teachers, as it is clear that teachers would hold opening or closing circles if they could (I surely would!). But the incessant rush of time-sensitive expectations combined with the demands on teachers to hit benchmarks prevents this from happening in many classrooms.[36]

This is an example of what can happen when teachers are given more

---

34 https://www.nytimes.com/2015/01/21/opinion/smartphones-dont-make-us-dumb. html?mcubz=0
35 Ibid.
36 https://www.youtube.com/watch?v=4UZ_lWr028o

time to build relational connections with students. Exercises like opening and closing circles should not be unusual. Students should view classrooms as incubators for learning – about content, curriculum, and self – in an environment that values time to reflect. Schools also should consider whether their daily schedule meets their school community's need for reflection time – particularly since students have a tendency to interact with their devices during lunch period or other free times.

I will conclude this chapter with an example not of a closing circle or of a Chapel or assembly, but of an opening circle. I spent several years working as an administrator at The John Thomas Dye School, a beautiful elementary school in Los Angeles. This elementary school was located high up in the hills of Bel Air, and the symbolism behind "reaching through the clouds" was taken literally when indeed clouds would settle below our campus, giving us the rare view of being atop a blanket covering the earth below us. It would be very easy for the children at this school to feel rarified (which they were) and act entitled (which they did not). One of the reasons why the school community propagated relational teaching is how it started the school day.

> Exercises like opening and closing circles should not be unusual. Students should view classrooms as incubators for learning – about content, curriculum, and self – in an environment that values time to reflect.

After drop-off, when teachers would stand in a row, greet the parent driving, and open the door for the students to funnel out, the entire community would come together in a semi-circle, facing the open view in front of them. On clear days, the cloud-blanket would be replaced with a 26-mile view, stretching out across Santa Monica and the Bay toward the outline of Catalina Island. Yet the kids rarely appreciated this blue-sky view. Rather, they benefitted by the view directly in front of them – their peers and teachers, all 400 of them, standing in a semi-circle, faces clearly visible.

Not only did this impressive visual support the notion that this was a relationally strong school. It was also what the students and teachers *did*. Every morning, they would recite a school pledge, which literally was the Sanskrit *Salutation of the Dawn*. For those who don't have it memorized like I do from 1,500 days of recitation, the mid-section states, "Yesterday is but a dream and tomorrow is only a vision. But today, well-lived, makes every yesterday a dream of happiness and every tomorrow a vision of hope." Every single morning, without fail, the entire community would come together and state this truth, which is essentially about valuing the present moment by letting yesterday retreat like a dream and visualize the possibilities the future holds. This is profound, mindful, meditative stuff – yet the young students and their teachers receive it on a deep level. This shared experience of Opening Circle centered the community for a few short yet stable minutes. It allowed everyone to put aside their immediate stresses, concerns, to-dos…and to come together in body, mind, and spirit and pledge to be present throughout the unfolding day ahead of them.

Every school should begin the day with such a high premium on community!

Some do, but many do not. The relational value is felt and understood by all – from the five-year-old kindergartener to the 75-year-old librarian. And I am certain that every day there existed a handful of children who counted on that moment as the one time of the day they would be *seen*.

Time to Look Within

The ideally relational school would contain time for reflection within the daily schedule. It would present meetings as opportunities for open sharing and receiving of ideas. It would view the student as an unfinished adult in the making who possesses an active inner life that is constantly interfacing with the natural world outside – in all its tangible, tactile, and experiential forms. Detracting from this vision is the "virtual world" that technology presents. Why have schools chosen to include an entirely additional world to their already over-packed real world experience during those precious minutes outside of class? By allowing technology to permeate the bricks and mortar world of students' sacred reflective time, schools are doing a disservice for the development of empathy, close relationships, and very possibly the optimal growth of the self.

Carol Becker, Dean of Columbia University School of the Arts in New York, New York, and author of *Thinking in Place: Art, Action, and Cultural Production*, writes in *Time* magazine about the need for reflection within public space. She asks, "What could better describe our contemporary situation than to say that the public sphere is no longer a place for collective action, but rather a dangerously redesigned network whose main function is to publicize the self?" When the public space is the high school quad, lunchroom, or student center, her question becomes an essential one. If our students are using free time to update their online presence, then the purpose of free time in school is being usurped. Their social skills development is being halted. Walk into most high school public spaces and you'll see a number of heads down, brows furrowed, thumbs sliding on the screens of devices aimed to produce dopamine hits with every ping. Says Becker, "As a result of our 'always-on' ethos, we have neither time nor space within which to lose ourselves in reflection. There is always something outside the self, robbing the self of the self."[37]

The ability to reflect has been identified in children as young as 20 months old, whose brains are developing at breakneck speed. Metacognition, the process of understanding one's own thought processes, is central to reflection in school. Why would we not give teachers the agency to prevent obstructions to students' metacognitive development?

Despite the connotation of being a relaxing process requiring very little energy, reflection in the classroom is active and multifaceted. For example, in the book, *Learning and Leading with Habits of Mind*, Arthur L. Costa and Bena Kallick define reflection in learning as a series of scaffolding actions. "To reflect, we must act upon and process the information, synthesizing and evaluating the data. In the end, reflecting also means applying what we've learned to contexts beyond the original situations in which we learned something."

> As a result of our 'always-on' ethos, we have neither time nor space within which to lose ourselves in reflection. There is always something outside the self, robbing the self of the self.

They continue, "In the reflective classroom, teachers invite students to make meaning from their experiences overtly in written and oral form. Reflective students know they can produce personal insight and learn from *all* their experiences."[38] In order to promote reflective student contributions in the classroom, expert teachers structure their classroom ethos so that everyone feels free to create and challenge hypotheses and insights.

Time for reflection outside of the classroom is also important for schools to encourage. Mr. Matthew ("Matt") Arnold is an educational technology consultant who has taught in several excellently regarded middle and high schools in his 15 years as an educator, including Crossroads School

---

37 http://time.com/4186034/technology-and-our-inner-lives/
38 http://www.ascd.org/publications/books/108008/chapters/Learning-Through-Reflection.aspx

Matt Arnold

and Harvard-Westlake School in Los Angeles and Latin School of Chicago. A certified yogi, film director and writer, Matt is a Renaissance man who has spent much of his energies developing a working philosophy on the integration of technology in schools. In his words, Matt prepares his students to "give them an efficient understanding of the use of digital tools combined with an awareness of the mindfulness needed to become balanced citizens of our future world." No small feat...yet he is doing this one school at a time.

At one point during our interview, Matt showed me a massive, leather-bound, time-worn journal from his years as a high school student. When he opened it, I was aghast at the amount of handwriting, article clippings, sketches and photos inside. It reminded me of a Kerouac or Ginsberg journal – stream of consciousness and deeply soulful, tangible and organic. When I asked him how he was able to fill it, he responded, "It was done in a completely reflective state. I would have an 11 o'clock class that ended at noon, and then I would have a one o'clock class, so I'd have a lunch hour. So I'd go grab a sandwich and sit in the student center and write for half an hour after interacting with my friends over lunch.

"The 'me' today would be doing the same thing, except he would be updating Facebook, looking at Snapchat, watching Instagram. This is a different type of reflection. The first main difference seems to be that journaling is an inward process. It is a reflective, connective experience done by ourselves, within ourselves. I often think about it as a process of learning about ourselves that was keenly helpful during our young adult years when we were discovering who we were becoming.

"Yet students journaling online today are keenly aware of its exposure to onlookers. That type of journal becomes a platform, and it is an outward process. The desire for external validation creeps in and casts its influence over the content of the topics being written about. We are living in a society governed by 'likes'. School, however, does not – should not – reinforce that."

Matt clarifies his point about inward versus externally aware reflection with the following: "What would be the opposite of social media validation would be self-driven reflection. It's about this whole theme of love, and people that seek love, and they seek attention and validation, instead of being in it and being self-reflective, and letting every moment inform who they are. The opposite is the temptation to go everywhere else, trying to find other people to define who you are." These are insightful words that parents, teachers, and other adults should keep in mind as they work with young people. Self-esteem comes from within.

> The 'me' today would be doing the same thing, except he would be updating Facebook, looking at Snapchat, watching Instagram. This is a different type of reflection.

As a technology director, his statements are both surprising and inspiring. Matt is not advocating abolishing technology in schools. Matt remains hugely enthusiastic about the power of technology to provide education to every person on the planet. Yet he is concerned when technology unnecessarily infiltrates the school culture during non-classroom times. He is drawing attention to the fact that many schools tend to take on technology without thinking about how it could impact the culture. He argues, "We're not going to move forward unless we become aware about how we're incorporating this technology, and just like there was physical fitness in the past, there needs to be this attention toward establishing technology wellness as part of every school's academic and social-emotional program."

In conclusion, relational schools allow teachers time to reflect in their classrooms, amongst their colleagues, and within themselves. Teachers are active learners. This time is not idle, although many in society believe it to be. All those weeks off in the summer don't measure up to frequent, consistent time to reflect in schools during the academic year. Students benefit from reflection time because it promotes deeper learning about the concept and themselves. Teachers benefit from the autonomy that comes with being permitted to incorporate a process that has proven positive effects toward the social, intellectual, and emotional state of their class. Schools benefit from a more mindful, less distractible student and faculty body.

Parker Palmer notes, "The salvation of this human world lies nowhere else than in the human heart, in the human power to reflect, in human meekness and in human responsibility."[39] There is power in reflection, and reflection time is essential to learning. Science has proven it to be so.

Recapping the Relational: Reasons to Reflect

In this chapter, the importance of reflection time was explored from many angles pertaining to the optimal classroom. Learning takes place when there is room for reflection after a lesson. Long-term retention cannot result from continuously receiving information. Our brains need time to synthesize. Whether it is through circling up to share the major lessons from the class period or journaling the events of the day, reflection time is key toward locking in the information and the lessons that experiences shape.

The relational teacher understands that the delivery of content is a give and take between her and her students. She is constantly receiving clues and cues from them in order to gauge whether to continue or to pause and ask, "are you following me here?" Learning is complex. The teacher who is compelled to rush through and put the finish line ahead of anything else has only completed her task at the base level. She has communicated but not taught. School schedules that allow time for teachers to collaborate and connect benefit from the collegial faculty that results. When schools have room in their weekly schedule for community gatherings such as Chapel, they are given the opportunity to strengthen their culture.

Students are figuring out who they are and whose they are. They are making meaning from their experiences through reflection. They are living in a world where information is at their fingertips, and stimulation is found by hitting the home button. Schools have an increasing responsibility to become havens for reflection and refuges from the constant overload of stimuli that exists at Volume Eleven in the world outside. When schools put more resources toward the relational and less toward the unnecessary technological, they can become refuges for growth and learning. When schools quiet down and prioritize reflection time, deeper learning and closer relationships – with others and with oneself – result.

39 Palmer, Parker (1998), *The Courage to Teach* (San Francisco: Jossey-Bass), p.21

Tom Fennel

Time to be authentic

"Teaching is a daily exercise in vulnerability."

Parker Palmer, *The Courage to Teach*[40]

"I tend, like most teachers, to think more about the things I do wrong, than the things that go right."

Colleen Kyle, History Teacher at Lakeside School, WA

Parker Palmer speaks of vulnerability as he reflects on how he felt after a particularly challenging and embarrassing classroom teaching experience. "I have reread and relived this miserable episode many times. What could I have done differently that might have made for a better outcome? But when I lead this exercise in workshops, I insist that participants avoid that question like the plague."[41] He encourages teachers to lean in to their mistakes, and view them not as suffocating failures but as learning experiences. He asks them to avoid finding "practical solutions" and instead burrow into the memory for insight.

Being a teacher means committing to a personal profession which brings you face to face with your own vulnerabilities as you stand and deliver in

40 Palmer, Parker (1998), *The Courage to Teach* (San Francisco: Jossey-Bass), p.17
41 Ibid, p. 74

front of a classroom of individuals. The relationship between teacher and student is based on learning expectations and predicated on connection. The more a teacher connects with their students, the better the probability the student will learn. Yet connection is not achieved merely through being kind, engaging, or theatrical. The deepest connections are formed through the exposure of vulnerabilities and honesty – the revelation of the true self.

Just as Holden Caulfield searched out the "phonies" in the adult world, today's students do the same. If childhood is learning how to own a world of imagination and play under the safe oversight of adults, the 'tween years and adolescence are the full ramp-up to the process of de-individuation. Separation from parents and identification with one's peers and other adult influences represent the classic definition of the teenage years. This is all good – albeit hard and at times heartbreaking for parents who have until this time been the object of their child's adoration and emulation.

Where do teachers fall into this world of transition, this world of growing up? They sit squarely in the middle. Yet the duration of this centering role can last 15 years or 15 seconds, depending on the authenticity the teacher presents. As a teacher, you are expected to know your material, control your class, communicate, assess, and inspire. Yet you are also trusted to discern what material to focus on or brush over, to plan assessments that reflect the content being studied, and to know the individual students in your care and not merely their grade point average in your class.

Students rightly take all of these responsibilities for granted. Of course they do. They are still growing up, and they expect the adults responsible for them to be looking out for them first and foremost. Yet they don't expect the teacher to be the perfect sage on the stage. Every student in the classroom is watching, listening, and intuiting the moment a teacher show signals of inauthenticity. The moment something a teacher says rings atonal – whether an utterance, reaction, or lack of response – they will register it. It might not be conscious. Indeed, it might be just a sense of quick disdain or a tweak of confusion swiftly replaced by the task at hand. Or it could be a brazen response, such as a question that comes off as a challenge, a crossing of arms and leaning back in the chair, or a quick turn to one's classmate with a whispered disparaging word or look.

Once a teacher commits the classroom sin of "do what I say, not as I do," he is toast. I frame it that way not to be blithe but instead to underscore how critical the student gaze can be. A revelation of hypocrisy can be a setback or a learning experience if responded to with sincerity.

Students forgive a teacher who momentarily appears inauthentic if he is already deemed trustworthy. When a teacher who has built trust states or does something incongruous with how his students have learned to view him, he is a curiosity, not a threat. Of course, this statement is true when focusing on minor examples of inauthenticity ("But you said the 2004 Red Sox were your favorite team of all time but now you say it's the 2007 Red Sox!"; "You told us this would be the easiest chapter in the book!"). In situations such as these, disconnection can create room for questions and lead to learning. There is nothing that brings a class into sharp, lean forward-in-the-desk focus than challenging a teacher over what he said earlier and how it conflicts with what he is saying now. This is grappling over inconsistency, not inauthenticity.

Inauthenticity can move into an uncomfortable middle zone, which is essentially being caught in a white lie. This is a wide zone, as it's the grey area between innocuous dichotomy and ethical irresponsibility. This is the zone where a teacher might state something as truth that earlier he'd stated wasn't. It's when a teacher teaches something incorrectly because he didn't have the courage to say, "I don't know." It's the teacher who states the paper will be returned on Monday, then Monday rolls around, and the papers are not returned.

> Once a teacher commits the classroom sin of "do what I say, not as I do," he is toast.

In all of these situations, the teacher response is critical toward whether he will regain authenticity with his students or lose it. If he states that he was incorrect about Pluto being a planet, he will regain trust – especially if he then teaches the correct information with passion and clear intent on fixing his mistake. If he states that he aimed at correcting all of the papers by Monday but didn't feel right only handing back half of the class's corrected papers, the class might understand. Things happen.

What is authenticity really? It's presenting oneself as fully human. It's sharing things that interest you. It's making your sense of humor known. It's setting up your moral spectrum of the classroom and the world around you. Authenticity is not catering to the student's moral relativism. It is not trying hard to be dialed in to pop culture to relate better to students. It is not being irresponsible with storytelling that is not relevant or age-appropriate to be thought of as cool.

Teaching is the lighting of fires of the spirit. It requires passion, commitment, integrity, and communication. The kindling is trust and safety. The importance of teachers connecting with students cannot be overstressed.

However, there are authentic ways to connect, and inauthentic ways to connect. Not everyone's favorite teacher will be the hip, witty actor with the charisma of a trained politician. But he will be for some. Not everyone's favorite teacher will be the introverted, sensitive yet distant teacher with the non-threatening academic persona. Yet he will be for some. Not everyone's favorite teacher will be the straight-laced, organized, strict teacher who rarely demonstrates warmth yet gets information across. Yet he will be for some.

Expert teachers don't enter the field to win a popularity contest – which is not to say there aren't some who enter teaching in order to redo high school. But those usually are not teachers who stick it out. If they do, they learn that retracing time is one of life's impossibilities, and that the reward from teaching comes in myriad forms – none involving being "cool at middle age."

The authentic teacher can be all the teachers described above. She can be strict, quirky, quiet, and hilarious – as long as she is authentically so. "Good teaching comes from the identity and integrity of the teacher," [42] writes Parker Palmer (who follows this up with one of the most pithy and perfect descriptions of a good teacher: "Good teaching comes from good people." [43]).

> Not everyone's favorite teacher will be the hip, witty actor with the charisma of a trained politician. But he will be for some.

There is an oft-stated piece of advice for new teachers: "Don't let them see you smile until January." This seems to be a universal way for a teacher to present herself two dimensionally, as a distant authority figure amidst her students. I am reminded of history teacher Colleen Kyle's analogy of a "full cup" from the chapter, "Time to Set the Dinner Table." It's better to start the year demonstrating genuine goodwill toward your students. In this way, the teacher is holding the bar high and students feel encouraged to maintain it. The teacher is authentically showing goodwill, and the students quickly learn to trust it.

But I also learned not to be dogmatic about the January rule. One October, I was walking down the hallway and Caitlyn, a young-looking 30-year-old 4th grade teacher, rushed up to me nearly crying with laughter. Caitlyn never cries. Caitlyn never laughs. I had no idea what had brought these emotions out.

"Follow me, Nat. We're dying here!"

I walked into her classroom, and watched kids literally rolling on the floor with laughter. Max was at the center of it, with the brightest, reddest face I'd

42 Palmer, Parker (1998), *The Courage to Teach* (San Francisco: Jossey-Bass), p.10
43 Ibid, p.13

ever seen on a child.

"Look!"

I looked away from the kids and onto the desks and the walls. There was blue inky liquid everywhere. Then I looked at Max. His hands were covered in blue.

I turned to Caitlyn. "His squeeze ball broke, didn't it?"

Caitlyn could barely answer my question, so I reasoned that this is exactly what had happened. When I saw Caitlyn at carpool a few hours later, I asked her about her mantra.

"What does this mean for your 'don't smile until January' rule? Halloween's still three weeks away."

"I think my mantra still works. I'm not changing it. But now, the kids know that I can laugh when the situation is as ridiculous as it was today. I'm only human. But I can get back to my persona tomorrow."

I thought about what she said, and it made sense. Caitlyn was not being inauthentic by keeping up this persona. In fact, the students saw more authenticity in Caitlyn after she went back to her persona because they saw that she values class discipline and structure. She willfully keeps herself a few (adult) steps removed from the student world in order to not blur it up for them (which can be confusing). She showed the students that they can be funny, that she has a sense of humor and therefore is not a robot, and that she can guide the class back to work again the next day – yet not as if nothing had happened.

The evening after Max burst his bubble, Caitlyn picked him up a new one – this time it was bright yellow – and handed it to him in front of the class first thing the next day. Then she began teaching again. Her actions were masterful. She showed that she remembered the incident, cared enough to buy Max a new squeeze ball, and had the expertise to steer the class back to work. She had that class in the palm of her hand.

Time to Teach in Technicolor

Another arena of teaching from a place of authenticity involves expressing genuine passion. I met Tom Fennell, a high school language teacher from Sierra Canyon School in Los Angeles, California, in 2004. While working at a new start-up school. Tom exhibits an underlying love for each and every one of his students, revealed by the depth of connection he generates. As a new, inexperienced Dean, I could always count on Tom to give me spontaneous, accurate feedback on any student.

During our interview, Tom recalled a teacher whose passion continues to influence his own teaching. "I remember those teachers whose passion inspired and moved me. I remember Paule Le Rider of the University of Paris. She taught medieval literature at Nanterre. Her specialty was folklore. I often think and am inspired by her passion about folktales. Her ability to read the stories to us passionately is a source of inspiration even today. I think of her often and wonder what became of her, not as a teacher but as a human being."

Decades after her class, Ms. Le Rider was remembered not for the details of her lessons, her assessments, or her areas of focus. Rather, she was remembered for her passion. The source of remembrance is a human one. Tom remembers the human being she was, not the genius she possessed. In that way, he learned about folktales in a deeply spiritual way. She taught her students with passion. Passion is energy. Energy is spirit. Spirit is teaching.

> Decades after her class, Ms. Le Rider was remembered not for the details of her lessons, her assessments, or her areas of focus. Rather, she was remembered for her passion.

Enrique Martinez Celaya, the world renowned painter and sculptor, recalls his first apprenticeship with a mentor who exuded passion in a similar manner to Ms. LeRider. Martínez Celaya shared, "At 12 years old, I apprenticed for a painter, Mayol. He loved painting! I learned countless lessons from back then. He gave lessons about technique. He was a methodical, traditional painter. The lessons were rigorous and not fun. Yet I connected with him because of his passion for his lessons. He was so excited about them – I became excited because he was excited. There was a life force in this guy – you could see his glow. He had wisdom from the way he worked."

You could see his glow. How many of us have basked in the glow of a teacher who is so deeply passionate about his craft that he literally glows? Enrique could sense this at 12 years old, and remembers it decades later. So many student groups I met with reiterated how they would work for a teacher, regardless of how strict or demanding, if that teacher had passion – and compassion.

Javier, a high school student from California, explains, "I think being passionate is more important than anything else. You care about what you're teaching. You get excited about what you're teaching. You're not bored with it, like a monotonous tone. The other thing, I think, is you understand the students, you feel for them. The teacher I'm thinking about actually fits both of those. What we would read in class, sometimes she'd literally cry when she was reading a sad part. Last year we were reading *Lord of the Flies*, and Piggy died. She started crying. She said she cries every time she reads that. Every time we would go to her class, it would be like a show. She was really passionate about what she was doing. She used to be an actress, I think, and so she'd captivate her students."

This teacher would *captivate* her students. Javier hit on something everyone can bring to the classroom, which is passion and compassion. Mr. Connolly possessed that "glow" when he taught Romantic Poetry. Nothing moved him more than Wordsworth's "Tintern Abbey" or Blake's "The Chimney Sweeper" or Coleridge's "Rime of the Ancient Mariner." As he recited these poems, his eyes gleamed and his voice wavered.

Enrique's painting mentor, Javier's English teacher, and my English teacher...all possessed passion and compassion. They exuded humanity and unabashed fearlessness in identifying the beauty in art. This authenticity reminds us that we are all connected through the intangible yet very true power that art commands. As Enrique observed, "How often do we see people love what they are doing? Mayol talked to himself while painting the lips of a commissioned piece." Mayol lost himself in the process of painting, as Javier's teacher lost herself in the high intensity of dramatic recitation, as Mr. Connolly lost himself in the words of the great Romantic poets.

Time to Be Seamless

One of the surest ways for a teacher to lose authenticity is to appear unpredictable. This isn't the same as deliberately choosing to throw a student off with a curveball question, giving a pop quiz, or tossing a lesson plan and focusing the class period on a completely unexpected topic. Rather, this is about appearing one way one day and completely differently the next day. This results in making trust difficult to achieve and connection distant. Remember the student Chloe's descriptive comment earlier, "I don't know which personality I'm going to get when I do (try to connect with her unpredictable English teacher)."

We crave consistency, and we can get thrown off when someone shows a side of himself we didn't know existed. However, we usually accept these surprises as expressions of a person's individuality, and feel relief that we're not all cookie-cutter creations, able to be labeled and "framed" after a five-minute conversation.

However, as discussed in the previous chapter, "Time to Get Organized", when it comes to teachers, success tends to fall upon those who are not just organized but also consistent. Just as a teacher is ill-advised to be the only "expert" in front of the classroom (this approach causes more distance than, say, being a confident partner in exploration), she is also advised to close the distance by being *real*. While teachers cannot – and should not – "let it all hang out" due to reasons of age-appropriateness and professionalism, teachers should be encouraged to be seamless in front of students. Being seamless is not synonymous with being peerless or flawless. Being seamless is closely related to being integrated. Integration is central to a teacher's strong sense of presentation.

> When it comes to teachers, success tends to fall upon those who are not just organized but also consistent.

Andy Barnett, the teacher and school pastor in Washington, D.C. who earlier shared the analogy of organized teachers to organized nurses, states, "The thing that sticks with me about teaching involves the integration of the divided life and undivided life. When living a divided life, it's like, "Behind the curtain is your personal life…money, romance, what you do with your free time…personal stuff. But in divided life, none of that stuff matters because you pull the curtain across and it leads to disaster." Andy asserts that it is this brokenness that is unhealthy when one is trying to present a strong self-concept. While it is possible to do this in certain professions, Andy asserts, "You can't keep the personal behind the curtain in teaching."

Why? It's because students learn from how we react, what we say, what we do, and what we deem important or unimportant. Students are seeking integration on a gut-level. They are sensitive to "surprises" ("You know what, I'm just not going to grade that test/paper/report after all"). They are attuned to nuance and they are hard-pressed when a teacher seems to turn on a dime. Teachers are expected to have bad days, to be tired, and to need another cup of coffee in order to function during the winter months. Yet they should build enough trust in their classroom environment that they are perceived by their students to be seamless and real.

Alan Rivera, the world language teacher at The Park School in Brookline, notes, "It's been 18 years of teaching, and the joy has expanded in me 20 times because I am encouraged to bring my whole and entire self to work every day. I am the exact same person I am standing in front of kids teaching as I am in front of my colleagues, as I am in front of my mother and father, as I am in front of you, as I am with the guy making my coffee."

Alan then makes a connection between building authentic relationships and building respect. "Because my identity is seamless, a relationship happens with my students. Respect builds because my students know I'm doing what I love and they know I'm being authentic. They know that the way I talk to them is the way I would talk to anybody else. In return, they get it. When I say that the joy is 20 times more, it's because it feels rewarding to be doing something that you care about and that you know your kids care about too. You can actually see it. By presenting an integrated and seamless sense of self, I absolutely strengthen the bond with my class."

Teaching in a school community that values the individuality of its teachers and students is a privilege that could be experienced by every teacher if administrators and school leaders opted to focus on it. Truly, who wouldn't want to be taught by Alan, who reveals his love for the content, students, and craft of teaching in an articulate and inspiring manner? Teach from the heart and the students will follow.

Time to Be Dignified

Dignity is a soft force communicated through speech, body language, and confidence. By choosing to create an optimal classroom, a teacher creates a haven that promotes the notion of building dignity. Yet a teacher cannot teach dignity if he feels his wings are being clipped. A teacher cannot inspire greatness from her students if she is communicating reticence and withholding her very identity.

Yarrott Benz, an art teacher from Sierra Canyon School in Chatsworth, observes, "So often kids don't connect with teachers because they don't view them as human. Connecting with high school kids requires a willingness to be really honest. Some teachers build interesting artifices or amusing personas around themselves, and kids often love that. However, I more admire the teachers who really connect on a human level."

One can't be a relational teacher if she is required to keep her identity in check in order to feel safe in her school culture (in which case, that teacher might want to migrate toward a more affirming school culture – a difficult decision yet many times a beneficial one). One cannot be a relational teacher if she feels blocked in by discrimination. Whether it is racial, ethnic, religious, gender or any other defining characteristic that defines a teacher, he or she is best served by being encouraged to authentically present him or herself in as honest and age-appropriate way.

This is not only because it would make him or her more fully human in the eyes of the students. It is also because the students look to their teachers as a portal to their future selves. If a teacher is not fully able to present *who* he or she *is* in the safely constructed, optimal confines of the classroom he or she *created*, then nobody thrives. Elementary school teacher Ros Won comments on this when she describes the importance of presenting herself not only as an expert teacher of elementary school students (and expert Nae-Nae dancer and water balloon fighter!) but also as a strong Asian-American woman.

"These kids need to see what a confident Asian woman/teacher looks like. Technology's not going to do that for them. I still need to represent. I need to be a role model for my Asian students, for them to see, 'Oh yeah, there's another Asian adult in my life here. I need to show other students who may not have Asian people in their life, 'Hey, this is what an Asian person looks like and does.' That really, I feel, is an important role for teachers, too, especially teachers of color. Technology does many things and opens many pathways to learning. Yet presenting myself and my Asian-American heritage is something a computer cannot do in my place."

> One can't be a relational teacher if she is required to keep her identity in check in order to feel safe in her school culture

Tracy Ainsworth, a history teacher at Philips Academy in Andover, Massachusetts, echoes Yarrott, "I think you get an authentic student-teacher connection when both the teacher and the student are able to regard one another as a full person and that a person isn't always succeeding but is, for the most part, always operating out of the good intention of wanting to succeed. I think you really have to care about your students and I think you have to engage with them way beyond just the subject matter that you're teaching that day. I always start my classes with what probably to an outsider would seem like casual small talk, even to the point of taking a few minutes more than I really need to, to do that before 'getting down to business.'"

Ironically, the "getting down to business" is exactly what Tracy is doing by taking the time to recognize the myriad dimensions of her students. The notion of being regarded "as a full person" requires openness and appropriate candor. In other words, it requires vulnerability and risk, with the presumption that both are regarded as strengths in an optimal classroom environment.

It also requires the clear delineation of roles. Students are looking for friendliness, not friendship from teachers. The difference is subtle, yet of tremendous importance. Friendship is predicated on trust and openness. Yet there are areas in a teacher's life that should not be open to students because they are not yet adults. They are on their way toward adulthood, yet they have neither the context nor the skills to wisely navigate the adult world.

When I brought up the notion of authenticity, Chatham Hall Rector and Head of School Suzanne Buck immediately focused on the important line between dignified and undignified authenticity.

"You need authenticity. Without authenticity, kids see through you. Whether it's an inquisitive kindergartener who tells it like she sees it, or a senior who is jaded, sarcastic and calling you out if you're not 100% forthright and honest, the students see through inauthenticity at any age. So much of it has got to be coming from a place of the kids recognizing who you are, and that you're willing to put yourself out there as a fully authentic adult mentor.

"It's really important as educators to establish appropriate boundaries, because we know what happens when boundaries aren't appropriate and the damage that can evoke. We have to balance between oversharing, and being overly guarded. Sometimes kids love when adults share something that's sacred with them. Some educators misuse that, and it can do damage to kids. It's about having appropriate boundaries while being appropriately authentic."

> The notion of being regarded "as a full person" requires openness and appropriate candor. In other words, it requires vulnerability and risk, with the presumption that both are regarded as strengths.

Suzanne continues, "As a leader, if I'm having a bad day, I'm not going to pretend that I'm not. It doesn't mean that I'm going to share the intricacies of what's going on, but I'm going to be honest and forthright and say, 'You know what? I'm having a tough day but I'm going to get through it,' and model how to appropriately be human. I think we have to demonstrate that it's okay to have vulnerabilities. Perfection doesn't exist, and perfection is really pernicious. Perfection within itself is not authentic, it's living up to somebody else's standards to try to achieve a certain status or accomplishment that's not altruistic. It doesn't stem from your own passion."

> As educators, we need to always reflect who we are and what we believe.

Suzanne completes her thoughts on authentic teaching with the following question: "Why should someone listen to us if we're not honest? As educators, we need to always reflect who we are and what we believe." Very true. The students would also agree.

Los Angeles-based actress and performing arts teacher Anneliese Euler tells a poignant story about her sophomore year high school biology teacher – the same one who did the letters project detailed earlier in this book.

"I don't remember the context for this, but at some point she told us that once upon a time, she got so discouraged that she took it out by kicking her own dog – who was at the wrong place at the wrong time – and immediately felt horrible about it.

"My memory on this is fuzzy. But somehow I got the message that it might be normal to feel really bad sometimes, so bad that you make a terrible choice. And then it might also be possible to admit it, make amends, forgive yourself, and move on. And that this depression I was feeling might one day pass. It was risky for her, as an authority figure, to reveal that.

"I think it gave me a glimpse of courage, vulnerability, the dropping of adult pretense, *oh, and by the way, we might not have to be defined by our lower selves*. I remember some students snickering about it afterwards, but I was grateful, maybe desperately grateful, for her opening up to us and displaying her fallibility. I think that thus far I had felt walloped by the unspoken message that what mattered was performance, achievement and getting things right. I was starving for adults to address matters of the spirit."

> I was starving for adults to address matters of the spirit.

I'll conclude this chapter with a beautiful quote from Chip Williams, the middle school teacher who moved back to teach in Los Angeles after teaching for many years in Turkey: "Kids see through inauthenticity like a glass window and that will fracture and as adults in their presence, we need to remember trust can't happen if they don't think you're authentic. Authenticity involves showing our humanity – oftentimes through humility and vulnerability. They don't necessarily need you to be the strong one that doesn't cry, but if you cry when they're crying – if you cry with them – they can trust you because they're on the same side. It comes back to incarnational stuff about speaking the same language. It's about identification, about recognizing underneath we're all the same, no matter how different we are. Let's go back to that essential proof about being human in our feelings."

Time to Be Generous with Humility

In his piece titled, "The Mental Virtues," *New York Times* columnist David Brooks credits professors Robert C. Roberts and W. Jay Wood for creating six "cerebral virtues" important to educators and leaders of groups. One of them is humility. Humility, Brooks explains, is "not letting your own desire

Anneliese Euler

for status get in the way of accuracy…the humble person fights against vanity and self-importance…such a person is open to learning from anyone at any stage of life."[44] This resonates with the examples from our expert teachers and artists. In each case, their own teachers helped them. Yet it is also true that the mentors received something from helping the student. And this successful connection, resulting in life-changing character growth, came about through the teacher's authentic communication with the student.

Students mentioned how they were hooked by their teachers' passion. As we read in the chapter, "Time to Teach in Technicolor," Javier recalls his English teacher's tears when reading aloud from *Lord of the Flies*. Indeed, it is the teachers who battle their ego and keep it at bay who tend to be open to authentic connection with their students. And it most certainly is the teacher who regards teaching as a relational, reciprocal endeavor who forges deep connections with her students. For a teacher to value his students' insights and thoughts, he requires an authentic appreciation for the students themselves.

David Brooks cites Roberts and Wood when he mentions another virtue of the mind: generosity. Generosity, he writes, "…starts with the willingness to share knowledge and give others credit. But it also means hearing others as they would like to be heard, looking for what each person has to teach and not looking to triumphantly pounce upon their errors."[45] Generosity is connected to humility here, as it involves empathy, which is the supreme act

---

44 https://www.nytimes.com/2014/08/29/opinion/david-brooks-the-mental-virtues.html?mcubz=0

45 https://www.nytimes.com/2014/08/29/opinion/david-brooks-the-mental-virtues.html?mcubz=0

of displacing one's ego with the experience of someone else.

Expert teachers exercise generosity with their feedback (verbal and non-verbal), and students respond to this feedback based on how authentic it is. The teacher who chooses to view each student answer as an opportunity to reinstate his position at the "head of the class" wins a pyrrhic victory: he gains the satisfaction of being "right," but loses the opportunity to forge a closer connection with students. As a result, the teacher ends up distancing himself from students. The class dynamic suffers as a result, as it becomes more about proving oneself right versus fostering a shared spirit of inquiry.

In *The Chronicle of Higher Education*, Rob Jenkins writes that "[Good teachers] seem comfortable in their own skin. Perhaps one reason students tend to like these faculty is that they like themselves, without being in love with the sound of their own voices. This is related to not taking themselves too seriously, but it goes beyond that. The root cause of bad teaching is a fundamental lack of self-confidence, leading teachers to overcompensate by being unreasonably demanding, aloof, or condescending to students. Paradoxically, professors who appear arrogant and narcissistic are often trying to cover up what they perceive as profound deficiencies in their own personalities and abilities. The best teachers are confident without being arrogant, authoritative without being condescending."

History teacher Colleen Kyle expertly juxtaposes the hierarchical and distant teacher-student relationship with the relational teacher-student relationship: one that is sensitive toward the fact that expert teachers work alongside their students, not from "on high." One that also recognizes that teaching students is teaching souls, each one comprising hopes, dreams, fears and anxieties. "There's a quote from the poem by Yeats, 'I've spread my dreams under your feet. Tread softly, for you tread on my dreams.' I don't think about that overtly, but that's what we have to do for a lot of these students who do see education as the essential way to succeed, whether with the few families who

116

haven't had college, or they're from families who are very, very driven for their students. The students are spreading a lot of dreams under their teacher's feet. We do need to tread softly for that reason."

When Colleen referenced this poem, I got the same goose bumps I felt when I first received it from my father after completing my first year of teaching. We must always dignify students' dreams – their hopes, expectations, and values. When students sense we are doing this, they speak of how "my teacher believes in me." This is not coming from the perspective of some 21st century self-help angle. Rather, it's the innate idea that youth are saturated by dreams and fears, and we as teachers must always remember this when we run our classes. If we are in tune with the spiritual inner lives of our students, we will find effective ways to engage and broaden their view of themselves and their world – through challenge, inquisitiveness, and understanding.

Colleen continues, "When I started working at my first school, there were a lot of cult of personality teachers. It's very fun and exciting to be around that kind of teacher, but I didn't want to be that way. I wanted to be the kind of teacher that created an environment where students thought their ideas were the most important in the room and not mine. If you are too overt, and put your own slant on things, the students won't go to certain areas, or certain directions with ideas. It feels really important to me that I do that, but there is a cost in terms of popularity, or the attention you get as a teacher, the recognition you might get in having accolades, or that kind of thing."

Again, this is the notion of humility being a strength. Teachers and students are embarking on a journey of exploration together. Whether students are learning the names of all of the colors of the rainbow in kindergarten or the Latin roots of English words in high school, recognizing each other's humanity is a central aspect of learning within the context of the teacher-student relationship.

The Archer School English teacher Jen Dohr speaks about the temptation to appear the expert in the classroom and how it works against the teacher because it reveals a lack of humility that is distancing. "This red flag situation takes place when you suddenly realize that you've somehow slipped into talking at your students. You are showing them what an expert in content you are. You know that *Odyssey* inside and out and you're talking about hyperbole and juxtaposition and…but all you're really doing is actually talking over them and showing off how brilliant you are." This is distancing because in a sense the teacher is using the content as a shield. The teacher knows the content inside and out, and that is obviously good. But the students don't. And when they sense that the teacher wants to pontificate instead of teach, the possibility for shutting down is high.

Jen says it best as she finds the silver lining: "Guess what, they're fourteen years old, and you've missed the entire point of teaching. It's so maddening but it's also so fun because if you realize you've missed the entire point of teaching, then there's hope." The call to reflect in order to cultivate hope is well-demonstrated in this example. Hope is a major element in personal growth. When a teacher realizes that he's crossed the line into "sage on the stage," he exhibits hope that comes with change.

> When they sense that the teacher wants to pontificate instead of teach, the possibility for shutting down is high.

But isn't it critical that students receive the most expert person guiding the classroom? Here, Jen defends the strength of not-knowing. "I'm not implying that content doesn't matter. Yes, of course it does. There is a great deal of flexibility that comes from knowing content, that comes from having a plan. You can only go off-plan when you have a plan. You can veer off of content when you know that content inside and out, forwards and backwards. That pontificating teacher who has that content, she can say to herself, 'I'm so glad I know all of that content so expertly. Now I will focus my growth on expertly knowing what teaching is, as well.'"

Paolo Freire elaborates on the intersection of dialogue and humility when he states, "Dialogue…is broken if the parties (or one of them) lack humility. How can I dialogue if I always project ignorance onto others and never perceive my own? How can I dialogue if I regard myself as a case apart from others – mere 'its' in whom I cannot recognize other 'I's?"[46] The trust-building teacher listens with ears and heart to the comments of students and comments coming from her own soul. An honest, vulnerable, and humble teacher will check herself constantly for her own innate biases – cultural, religious, or ethical – and she will listen for bias in her students as well. This constant action requires time.

Freire makes the argument that it is only with continuous reminders of her own humanity that a classroom teacher can maintain trust with her students. We are teachers with souls, who teach to souls. Humility makes possible the safe sharing of ideas, perspectives, and insights that serve to bring a classroom together in the spirit of learning. We teach because we are growing learners ourselves, informed by the adult wisdom that tells us it's okay to not-know.

In 21st century teaching, the answers are ascertainable with a few keystrokes. Consequently, the role of a teacher is to help guide students to

---

46 Ibid.

an answer through asking the right questions and advocating for a spirit of inquiry in the classroom. This should be a boon to the profession, and hardly a slight. Expert relational teachers are passionate about their content area, yet very few would state that they know "everything." Besides, knowing is only part of the job expectation; expert teaching is based on how well material is conveyed.

> At some point I came to recognize that teenagers want to be taken seriously and they want to be valued and that my people skills were vital.

History teacher Todd Whitten reflects on his early years of teaching and how he grew into an expert teacher once he resigned himself to the fact that he would never be a perfect expert on content.

"Over and over, when I started teaching, I wasn't an expert in the subject, couldn't have been. You can't be a world history teacher and know everything. I'm still not, but over time I realized that I was good at connecting with people. I would come into the classroom with these somewhat rudimentary people skills and I would build upon them as I simultaneously built upon my content knowledge. Over time, I grew and at some point I came to recognize that teenagers want to be taken seriously and they want to be valued and that my people skills were vital. I recognized that I was in this incredibly powerful position of seeing my students and that connecting was actually more important than content when it comes to learning."

English teacher Rob Crawford speaks about the power of vulnerability in the classroom, and how sharing that he doesn't know everything about the subject being taught can be viewed as a bonding moment based on trust. The teacher trusts the students to understand that he is not a computer. The students trust the teacher to be giving his best at instructional delivery, and that his not-knowing is not a sign of ineffectiveness but rather an open door to shared discovery.

"I think this is another way to build trust – to help the students realize that the teacher is the student too. We're all students. I sometimes will say, 'I read this passage and I'm actually not sure what's happening here. I knew you guys would help me understand this. Can you guys all turn to page 277 and line 120. John, will you read?' I'll say, 'What's going on here?' They know I'm not just baiting them. I literally am not sure what's happening here. They'll have different opinions. I'll say, 'Know what? Now I understand much better, thank you.'

"I told them, 'I know all of you are taking a Classics course right now and have taken two or three years of Latin. I know there are going to be moments when I'm going to pronounce a name wrong, or I'm not going to know what a Latin word means. I know there are going to be moments when my ignorance is going to be exposed. I am not an expert on this text and we're learning it together.' Instant trust and respect. Not-knowing is definitely an asset and a teaching tool, to tell you the truth."

The content is there to serve the teaching.

We want students to be comfortable taking chances in school. We want curiosity to be embraced, and the pursuit of inquiry to be held to the highest level. When a teacher models not-knowing as empowering (and human), then his students are free to not-know themselves…and take on the human pursuit of knowledge-seeking, which is at the heart of all excellent classrooms.

English teacher Jen Dohr corroborates Rob's example about not-knowing as an asset when she speaks about the role of content as it relates to optimal teaching. "The content is there to serve the teaching. I see it being placed as the end goal, especially by younger teachers who are proving themselves in the field. Yet it is absolutely there to serve (what's most important), which is the learning." The expert teachers interviewed for this book uniformly speak about the importance of knowing their content matter (and they all do – which is why they are able to so clearly articulate the relational approaches they take). Yet when students understand that it's not through laziness or carelessness that a teacher "not-knows," the act of being fallible with content presents itself as strength in humility.

Through Todd's early years of teaching, he recognized the impossibility of being the expert on everything – and a broader definition of what a teacher really is. Through the realization that expert teachers teach learning, Rob was able to unite his class around a shared search for knowledge. Lastly, through placing the content "in the end goal," Jen was able to narrow her focus and execute the best strategy to get her class to score. All of these examples recognize that learning is not consistent and impossible to codify. Yet this fact is exactly what makes teaching a human profession. We teach learning so that we grow as people, in all of our fallible ways.

Time to Challenge

I remember standing in front of parents at the beginning of school one year, when I decided to take a chance. Perhaps it was because we were fresh from summer, still feeling the glow of sun on our skin and relaxation in our muscles from time away. Perhaps it was the positive vibes in the assembly hall

– the Parent Association President gave a rousing speech about the constant need for parent volunteers, the Auction Committee gave their annual pitch regarding the year's Special Event and Auction, and the coffee was especially tasty.

"School," I began when I got up to make my speech to all of the fresh-faced, eager, smiling parents, "is not always going to be easy. In fact, learning is hard." At that comment, everyone grew silent. Knowing I struck a nerve, I persevered, "Learning doesn't come with ease. It is only through struggle that learning takes place." This was not what they wanted to hear. I had crossed a line.

But I knew I had back-up. Paul Tough, in his book *How Children Succeed*, states that "Learning is hard. True, learning is fun, exhilarating and gratifying – but it is also often daunting, exhausting and sometimes discouraging."[47] Tough makes the point that challenge is a key component to deep learning. The opposite is true as well; without challenge, a student becomes passive to new information and it doesn't stick.

There has been much written in recent years regarding effort and hard work in school. Paul Tough's *How Children Succeed* and Angela Duckworth's *Grit* use scientific research as well as anecdotal evidence to impart the simple message that learning is hard. Amy Chua's *The Battle Hymn of the Tiger Mother* adds a personal spin to the topic.

But learning *is* hard. Still, the number one parent complaint I hear is, "My child isn't having fun in school." Have we been conditioned to view school through the lens of fun versus the lens of real life? Have we adopted school as a safe zone for our children, where any sort of stress should be removed? Have we decided that teachers need to be advocates only – and not be given the authority to actually teach?

As history teacher Todd Whitten elaborates, "School is supposed to be hard. Learning is not supposed to be easy. But if school is hard and learning is difficult, and you're a teenager, it's super easy to fall to the temptation of saying, 'I'm not doing it. I can't do it. I can't. I won't.' All of those check-out words get used."

I've witnessed that during the first few months of a school year, students and teachers come together and – in optimally relational classrooms – develop bonds of trust and connection steeped in authenticity. They engage in work and grapple in the grey. For the first few months of school, assessments and feedback are fairly easily given and received. Students work for their teachers; teachers work for their students. A healthy, symbiotic relationship is developed

47 Tough, Paul (2012), *How Children Succeed* (London: Arrow Books: Random House), p.61

and growth begins. This amazing period of transparent feedback both given and received is short-lived, however, because by the end of the first two or three months, report cards typically come out, and school often becomes defined by competition based on comparison.

> If school is hard and learning is difficult, and you're a teenager, it's super easy to fall to the temptation of saying, 'I'm not doing it. I can't do it. I can't. I won't.' All of those check-out words get used.

Mark Twain famously stated, "Comparison is the death of joy."[48]

This isn't the challenge we need in schools. Challenge is not about competition with anyone except oneself. Even a 3rd grader knows this. I was sitting at lunch with a table of 3rd graders and I asked them what a good teacher does. "Easy," stated Franklin. "A teacher teaches us how to learn." Impressed, I followed up with, "How do you learn? Is it against your friends in the classroom?" Franklin looked at me incredulously. "No! It's against yourself." I looked around the table. All the 3rd graders were nodding in time with chewing their Tater Tots. I was nodding as well, in double-time!

Honest feedback is at the heart of impactful learning. Students will not accept challenge without feedback. Feedback could come the form of summative assessments or letter grades. Feedback could come in the form of teacher-set expectations and teacher-communicated critiques on how those expectations were met.

Teachers are in charge of the learning process for their students (often averaging 25 of them – per section) over the course of nine months. They prep, teach, assess, rinse, lather and repeat for eight hours a day, five days a week – at a minimum.

We all want teachers to feel impassioned, emboldened, confident, secure, and moving with momentum. History teacher Todd Whitten says, "In today's society, we as teachers spend more time with the kids than the parents do. Kids don't have dinner with their parents every night. They're not sitting around the table talking about their day anymore. It's a meal on your own or it's something on the fly. That's sort of the way our world works. To have another adult in the course of your day compliment you on something you did, or even just *notice* that you did something is hugely powerful. It's

48 https://www.goodreads.com/quotes/548857-comparison-is-the-death-of-joy

tremendously motivating. We're social creatures."

In conclusion, Todd continues, "If the student trusts me, if she feels that I'm on her side, if she feels that I *know* her, she will work for me. I can go to that student and say, 'Yeah, you didn't do well. I'm not going to sugarcoat this, you didn't do well on this assignment, but here are three ways you can do it better.' If I have connected with her, and she thinks, 'Yeah, Mr. Whitten knows me', it becomes such an easy conversation, and it becomes so simple to then have the student respond like, 'All right, I'll try again.'"

Todd is right. Children absorb a teacher's energy and ethics through their pores. A teacher's ability to challenge is relationally based, however, because the student who feels "noticed" is a student who will more likely listen to the critical feedback from the teacher.

Time to Be Happy

"What is the difference between happiness and pleasure?" I asked.
"Happiness is peace," one student answered. We discussed how desire arouses restlessness, how desirelessness unveils abiding inner peace.
"Some pleasures can destroy you," a young man said.
In the end a young woman observed, "Pleasure is only temporary."
In this lesson, we learned a new vocabulary word: *contentment.*

Middle School teacher Robert "Chip" Williams

I am writing this chapter on National Teacher Appreciation Day. This is a day (now a week that should be a year) designed to recognize the hard work teachers put into their craft. I always wondered about the timing of this recognition. I believe a teacher must have advocated for it being in May because, despite spring being about renewal, for a teacher it might as well be autumn. Energy levels are diminishing, coffee makers are overheating, and the faculty room walls are covering their ears. Of all times of the year, spring requires an extra boost.

We all want to be happy at work, in marriages, friendships, and partnerships, and with ourselves. Happiness is the subject of the positive psychology movement, which emerged from the brilliant idea of focusing not on what makes us all messed up and conflicted (i.e., pained), but instead on what makes us feel good. That's it. Inversion of the paradigm. The results have had major effects on the way we live our lives today. And they've benefitted the way we teach students as well.

Studies have proved so much about the power of positive thinking.

They've revealed how positive self-esteem leads to strength and grit, and how removing the "electron cloud" of anxiety opens channels for long-term retention.

Happiness is a strong sense of well-being. Being happy is essential for teachers to be most effective in creating optimal learning environments. We can all relate to when our sense of well-being has been strong, such as when we've received praise from our administrator, run our first marathon, passed the test, aced the serve, or fixed the faucet. Happiness is all of that.

I've noted several times that learning is hard. Fortunately for all of us with a limited reserve in our extraversion tank, learning takes place with all types of caring and trustworthy teachers. Are these teachers making students happy all the time? Are they fonts of knowledge or fountains of gushing Technicolor praise? We cannot expect teachers to be unconditionally happy – for good reason. They need to challenge, assess, critique, and offer substantial feedback to their students. This is where happiness comes in.

To be not only effective but excellent, relational teachers possess a healthy sense of well-being that goes beyond feeling safe in school.

Parker Palmer writes, ""Relational trust – between teachers and administrators, teachers and teachers, and teachers and parents – has the power to offset external factors that are normally thought to be the primary determinants of a school's capacity to serve students well."[49] To be not only effective but excellent, relational teachers possess a healthy sense of well-being that goes beyond feeling safe in school (also important). They exude validation that comes from within. In order to feel validated within, a teacher is made to feel validated from the outside as well. This validation comes from a day-to-day feeling of respect and support. Does an administrator swing through the class on a regular basis, even if a teacher is doing "a great job?" Does she attend special class events? Does she respond to emails in a timely manner, putting the temptation to radiate busyness aside in order to forge closer bonds with the teacher?

A teacher exuding a strong sense of well-being is a strong teacher. Just as students can sniff hypocrisy and inauthenticity, they can also sense weakness and cowardice. Well-being communicates to students that you're pleased with your place in the classroom and the school as a whole. Well-being is at the core of an expert teacher's persona.

49 Palmer, Parker (1998), *The Courage to Teach* (San Francisco: Jossey-Bass), p.xvi

Martin Seligman, the founder of positive psychology, explains, "Unlike the negative, firefighting emotions, which identify, isolate, and combat external irritants, the positive emotions broaden and build abiding psychological resources that we can call on later in life."[50] A strong sense of well-being strengthens character. It eliminates the energy-sapping stress that affects anyone who is constantly on guard, always feeling "negative, firefighting emotions." When one is constantly on the defensive, with their shields up and masks on, they are not projecting an authentic and open self. The ability to connect is significantly impaired.

A strong sense of well-being also opens the gateway for better relational teaching and learning. Seligman states, "Positive mood produces broader attention, more creative thinking, and more holistic thinking."[51] Think about it. When you're feeling resentful that you're not getting recognized for the job you're doing, or when you're stressed out about the unregulated busy work falling on you from the offices on high, you're not going to respond to a student's burst squeeze ball with uncontrollable laughter, are you? When you are feeling secure, appreciated, and "good enough" (knowing that delirious happiness is infrequent and quite off-putting to students in your charge), you see the student's squeeze ball explode in bright blue colors all over the classroom and the last response you consider giving is a reprimand. It's random, it's funny, and it's completely not intentional. It's theatre, and you respond to it with good humor.

> An equally important lesson was learned as well, which is that to laugh is to be human.

In responding to the constant yet each time unexpected, random student events, such as a desk chair pushed back too far or a completely screwy answer or a loud emission of gas from either top or bottom, laughter might often be the best response. This isn't to say it's the only response. During the squeeze ball event, the student was instructed to clean his mess and apologize to the class for his distraction. Yet an equally important lesson was learned as well, which is that to laugh is to be human.

When your sense of well-being is strong, you are more open – open to tracking the circuitous path in which a student is heading, stepping into the shoes that guided a student to an incorrect answer, and to torching a lesson plan in order to blaze a new way of thought.

50 Seligman, Martin E. P. (2011), *Flourish* (New York: Free Press: Simon & Schuster) p.66
51 Ibid, p.80

Time to See Ourselves in Others

Middle School teacher Chip Williams recognizes the importance of remembering who we are when we teach. Like Parker Palmer, he asserts that the undivided self makes the best teacher. Yet Chip also recognizes that through teaching, he learns more about himself. As unfinished selves, we place ourselves in the fertile environment of the classroom. Reasonably, much of our focus is on the growth of the students. Yet Chip recognizes that through teaching others, one gains a greater understanding of self.

"Essential teaching is: See God in each other. When you look into another's eyes, you see the light of God, the light of the self. *Atman* [Sanskrit: the essential self]. The light in your eyes, in the eyes of others, it's the same light.

When I look at my students, I see a reflection of myself.

When I look into my students' eyes, they are not separate from me. When I look at my students, I see a reflection of myself in that little chubby girl who giggles all the time. In that boy who slams the door behind him and is full of bravado. They are all part of me. I don't feel separate from my students – or anybody, really – I feel a kinship instead. My students know that I 'see' who they are and I accept them no matter what. There's a sense of feeling recognized, seen, accepted and welcomed."

This is reminiscent of history teacher Colleen Kyle's earlier line, "I see you, I hear you, I trust you." When students are seen for who they really are – warts and all – and they continue to be affirmed and acknowledged for their efforts, they feel believed in. This belief is impossible to fabricate. Students know when their teacher has hope for them, and they know when their teacher has given up on them. When they feel truly seen is when they feel the fuel of true belief.

Chip explains, "I'm 55 years old, but I was 7 years old, and that 7-year-old still exists in me, the 14-year-old, the 22-year-old also still exists in me. And I can access that stage of my being. It's still alive in me. So when I'm talking with a 5th grader, I can enjoy the fascination, the playfulness, the being silly. But when I need to be the adult, I'm the adult. My students in Turkey would always say, 'Man, you're 55, but you're so young!' It's like the Russian matryoshka dolls – I share my energy from whatever layer is being communicated. Whatever age is being channeled through the classroom experience at the present time."

You can't get more authentic than that. The idea of teaching as reaching into the historic layers of our past selves is fascinating. Besides Russian dolls, I think about sedimentary layers of the Grand Canyon or the rings in the tree

Chip Williams

trunk. *The Giving Tree* by Shel Silverstein comes to mind as I consider the impact of wisdom that only years behind us can provide, and how teaching calls us to reconnect with those years as a way to effectively connect with students.

As we get older, our students relate to us differently. Like the aging process in its entirety, it is important that we embrace our accumulating years. I've lived in Los Angeles long enough to witness the tragedy that happens when a person decides to undergo deep levels of surface change in vainglorious efforts to slow down or stop the inevitable. With teaching, there is an ironic juxtaposition between it keeping us young ("Man, you're 55, but you're so young!") while forcing us to recognize our getting older as our students relate to us differently.

Jamie Neilson, the Upper School Director at The Episcopal School of Los Angeles, puts it wisely, "Definitely there are teachers who come to it right out of college and they're good. They're naturals and they have connection that kind of comes from their youth and their energy. However, I feel like you see people in their late twenties, their early thirties, coming to this point where that automatic connection that used to kick in every year in the beginning of the year, isn't kicking in anymore because they are becoming older. The kids look at them and they see old. They go from being the shiny apple to being the harvester."

I went through that process. At 22, I started out as a young teacher eight years older than his youngest student. I was like an older cousin to them. By the time I hit 32, I noticed that students were treating me more like an adult relative, an uncle. Once I hit 40, I was absolutely viewed as a father figure. The way they spoke changed in tone; the way they addressed me changed in formality. This has nothing to do with respect or earned validation. It was truly because I was appearing older – I *was* older – and they reflected this as clearly as Dorian Gray's mirror. I often hear from teachers that this transition is a relief. They are no longer interrogated about their social lives, their personal lives, and their private lives. They are regarded as of a separate generation, one that is unlike theirs – as it should be.

Parker Palmer quotes Erik Erikson when he says that, "In midlife we face a choice between 'stagnation' and 'generativity.'" He defines the terms by stating, "Stagnation is the state chosen by teachers who are so threatened by students that they barricade themselves behind their credentials, their podiums, their status, their research." Palmer adds, "It is not unusual to see faculty in midcareer don the armor of cynicism against students, education, and any sign of hope. It's the cynicism that comes when the high hopes one once had for teaching have been dashed by experience...I am always impressed by the intensity of this cynicism, for behind it I feel the intensity of the hopes that brought these faculty into teaching."[52] Wow. Here, Palmer equates the intensity of optimism one feels as a young teacher with the intensity of pessimism one feels at midlife. The solution, Palmer asserts, can be found in generativity.

They go from being the shiny apple to being the harvester.

"On one hand, [generativity] suggests *creativity*, the ongoing possibility that no matter our age, we can help co-create the world. On the other hand, it suggests the endless emergence of the *generations*, with its implied imperative that the elders look back toward the young and help them find a future that the elders will not see."[53] This is an altruism-based definition. Palmer is viewing the elder teacher as someone with power to create a robust future through conveying this power to the younger generation. There is sacrifice in this – as Palmer writes, the teacher will not necessarily see the outcome of his creative-based power transference. Yet there is something to be said about faith here. We rarely know how we impress people. The letters or emails or phone calls received from long-ago students are rare, yet each one poignant. Those, however, are not the benchmarks heralding a job well-done. Rather, this sense of accomplishment comes from within. As much as

---

52 Palmer, Parker (1998), *The Courage to Teach* (San Francisco: Jossey-Bass), p.49
53 Ibid.

we focus on developing intrinsic motivation in our students, we must do so within ourselves as well. The letters are nice to receive, yet they are not accurate measurements of the positive impact we have had on the river of students who have entered and exited our classrooms.

Palmer continues, "There are great gaps between [the elder teacher and the student]. But no matter how wide and perilous they may be, I am committed to bridging them – not only because you need me to help you on your way but also because I need your insight and energy to help renew my own life."[54] What raw vulnerability! Palmer captures the power of teacher and student so clearly in this explanation of how generativity can eradicate stagnation. By understanding the role both play in the classroom dynamic, the teacher can be open to learning new ways of thought from the student.

This theme of "teacher as learner" is addressed in many of my interviews with expert teachers. It is a key reason why expert teachers remain in the field.

Chip Williams concludes, "Teaching is always accompanied by wisdom and maturity. With the knowledge and recall of your mindset at 16 years old, say, this ability to teach is enhanced. Excellent teaching is a spiritual endeavor, and it involves tapping into the spiritual self and the multiple selves we all still inhabit from our past. There is a lot of spirituality in teaching. It's a calling. Our students relate to us, and we relate to them. Yet we are not 20 years old anymore. We are respected and revered as the teacher possessing life experiences that the students in front of us only wish they too can have as well."

> As much as we focus on developing intrinsic motivation in our students, we must do so within ourselves as well.

This is a critical description of the generative transference between the authentic teacher and student. The teacher standing and delivering in front of the classroom feels trusted (and trusting), connective, authentic and secure in the fact that he has benefitted from time to reflect. With these relational elements in play, expert teachers know that they can lead through *who* they are. They can inspire simply by *being*. As Chip mentions, students understand that their teachers have lived decades beyond their own. In the optimal classroom, the authentic teacher demonstrates solid character values and his ethical compass is set north. When this happens, a teacher is prone to being emulated as a beacon of hope. "I've lived these experiences and

54 Ibid.

now I am giving back in hopes that you benefit from them as well," the teacher says through his actions. Students pick up on this, and they prepare themselves for exploration – of curriculum, yes, but also of present-day and (more excitedly) future self-concept.

Recapping the Relational: Aiming for Authenticity

We teach in order to learn. We facilitate learning in our students as well as in ourselves. When it comes to the lessons, we learn more about ourselves when in front of the classroom than we tend to recognize. We see ourselves through the mirrors being held up to us by our students. The furrowed brow when we say something that doesn't compute. The stifled chuckle when we do something funny. The raised eyebrows when we are being unfair. As teachers, we are receiving feedback while giving our lesson. This dynamic is non-verbal and sometimes hard to discern. Yet the cues are there for those brave enough to seek them out.

Authenticity is an important element toward building a relationally strong classroom. Being authentic is based on being a real human being in front of the youth in your charge. It is about exhibiting understandable, relatable human reactions in the varied situations that take place throughout the classroom period. It is not the same as being an open book. This distinction is an important one, as some teachers feel that the best way to connect with their students is to share everything about themselves. This is not what we expect from the adult in the classroom. There is a constant need to honor the world of the young and not to taint it due to a selfish need to overshare.

Schools provide opportunities for students to observe and interact with adults in meaningful ways that inform them of the type of adult they see themselves becoming. Students are exposed to the wide variety of personalities that comprise teachers. They understand that there is no one type of teacher and they learn how to respond to the different types of adult personalities that guide them down their educational path. They also might see themselves in their teacher – their identities displayed in front of them. When this happens, a stronger self-concept results.

Students are deeply motivated when they witness their teacher "lit up" about the subject matter being taught. Passion absolutely matters, as students are taken in by it. Teaching in Technicolor provides students with an example of what happens when someone is truly in the flow – and how captivating it is to bear witness to it. The honesty that comes with witnessing a person truly in their element is juxtaposed by the distancing that occurs when a person is not authentic. When a teacher is hypocritical and appears one way but acts another…those traits rarely serve toward creating a strong relational classroom.

As Chip Williams stated, "Trust can't happen if [the students] don't think you're authentic."

Cara DeCarlow, a world languages teacher at Sierra Canyon School in Los Angeles, California, elaborates on the benefits of being seen by one's students as an authentic teacher. She states, "I think it's great when students see a different side of you as a teacher, like on school trips, retreats, and events outside the school day. They see you in a different context and that's what makes the relationship stronger, because they're seeing you as you really are, in different moods and mindsets. For example, they see you on freshman retreat and you're like, 'It's hot and I'm sleeping in a tent – and I'm not happy right now. And I need my coffee!' And they can relate to that. They can relate to you in a different way. They see your humanness." By seeing our humanness, they see us as we really are. The time required to be authentic sometimes means taking time out of the regular school day (or work hours) in order to share your human self while they, too, share more of theirs.

You Are The Geography Teacher!

...partake in an ongoing project. Basically, what you will do is... research a facet of geography and how it influenced an ancient ...ce you've completed research, you will teach your classmates ...We want you to grapple with the information. Question it. Break it ...r about it. Then put your ideas down on paper and present them to

...to what we have learned about culture and geography this year ...social studies curriculum, discussions... even the books you have ...e discussed how geography affects culture, but now you will study ...n an ancient civilization with the pur... ...understanding how ...d and created its identity. You... ...an expert in this field ...information to yo...

...ng ancient Rome, discussing the villa and

...ding: Was it obvious that you really questioned this passage ...deeply about it and what it meant?

...ation: Did you get to know the geography well? Did you do ...earch? Did you consider more than one piece of information? ...y discrepancies in your research (conflicting information)?

Liz Ganem

5

Time to explore

"The eye – it cannot choose but see;
We cannot bid the ear be still;
Our bodies feel, where'er they be,
Against or with our will"

William Wordsworth, "Lyrical Ballads"

I write this chapter from the Yorkshire Dales, England, which is an area famous for its medieval history, sheep, and natural beauty – the selling point for the coast-to-coast walk bisecting this area of northern England. Through rolling pastures, haunting woods, and along a rushing riverside, I have traced century-old stone walls and crossed bridges of similar age. The weather is "all four seasons in a day," however, and I find myself constantly layering and disrobing and attempting to ignore my wet, cold and squishy feet in my not-100% waterproof boots. Despite this, I have found that walking alone in nature has the power to facilitate deep thinking and inspire unexpected thoughts, ideas, and even the rare epiphany.

Like with these medieval forests in northern England, the classroom also holds limitless opportunities for individual and shared exploration. Like the ever-shifting physical environment, the classroom is prone to varying barometric pressures. Unpredictability reigns. Yet through this imperfection, the optimal teacher forges ahead in their eternal quest to make exploration engaging and boundless. In the relational classroom, exploration is an essential element of teaching and learning. Expert teachers encourage student exploration. Students expect that teachers have explored the outer limits of their content areas. Parents hope their children come alive in classroom environments that celebrate imagination and reward exploration. Perhaps the rare epiphany will take place for them as well.

Exploration requires safety and risk-taking. Students need to be given permission to explore the intrinsic drive of an author, the trajectory of a comet circling the sun, or the different formulae that result in the right answer for a puzzling math problem.

When students explore in partners, small groups, or whole classrooms, amazing things can result. Yet these results can only take place when listening skills and proper communication etiquette have been addressed. How do we foster free exploration when we also need to be comfortable with advice and critique? How can we maintain the safety of free exploration while also communicating that the path a student is going down is a rabbit hole and the mission of his imagination or discovery must be arrested?

> How often have we seen a student approach his teacher with pride in his exploration, and have the teacher return the enthusiasm with that of her own?

In the presence of a teacher who truly knows where a student is coming from in his pursuit of inquiry, magic and brilliance can be the result. How often have we seen a student approach his teacher with pride in his exploration, and have the teacher return the enthusiasm with that of her own? The bounce in the student's step, the ear-to-ear grin, and the shine in his eyes all communicate growth. The student has set out to explore a topic or question, and he has received not only the affirmation from his teacher, but a sense of pride and recognition for his work. This is the glue of student-teacher relationships. Exploration is based on mutual understanding and respect for work and effort the student invested.

Maintaining an exploration-based classroom builds trust in students to utilize their own time. In an exploration-based classroom, teacher guidance is minimal, as the focus of the class is student-directed. They learn from their peers, control their sense of understanding, and grow in their sense of agency. All together, these traits combine to build a stronger sense of competency.

The teacher gives students freedom to probe deeply into a topic. She is watching out of her own sense of curiosity about the topic being explored and about her students. She is curious about how students are grasping the concept. She is curious about students' questions about the concept. She is curious about how students proceed in digging deeply into the concept. If students are working with others, she is curious about how they are working. Are they team-focused? Are they leaders? Followers? Extroverted? Introverted? Even as 5-year-olds, students sense these things, and they feel secure to continue exploring, knowing that they are being observed with care and hope.

And observe she must. Adrienne Agena, a 20-year kindergarten teacher now admissions director at Brentwood School in Los Angeles, California, states, "The risk of exploration takes place when the kids don't feel confident and there is no guidance from an adult." Conversely, there is a risk in being too vocal as an adult, the authority figure wielding a huge influence in the classroom.

Adrienne continues, "There exists a fine line between free time and guided exploration. Most of the learning and growing comes from exploration, yet it is important to define the task at hand, give background information, model if possible and extract info as the kids come up with it." These guidelines can be applied to K–12 students of any age. Clarity of the topic, context shaping the topic, modeling, and drawing from student input are all key components of organized instruction.

> Under the watch of a vigilant teacher, kids feel confident, comfortable and secure.

Clarity of instruction and definition of the task at hand is not only of central importance when teaching kindergarteners, it's also key for teachers at all levels of the K–12 learning community. Mariale M. Hardiman states, "Teachers must…be cognizant of the stress created by seemingly benign practices. For example, teachers can create stress for students by issuing unclear directions for performance, either through poorly designed written assignments or indirect 'veiled commands' that disguise a teacher's true intent."[55]

As motivators, Adrienne states, "Kids get each other excited. That's one of the reasons why it's valuable to share what they learned with each other. Individual exploration is harder at the younger age when there is a guided lesson that is taking place because the kids haven't had years of socialization. On the other hand, it is important for children to be given opportunities for making choices, exploring and feeling comfortable taking risks in their learning – this is, I believe, essential for their growth. With exploration,

---

55 Hardiman, Mariale M. (2003), *Connecting Brain Research with Effective Teaching* (New York: Rowman & Littlefield Education), p.31

students are given tools that encourage freedom. Under the watch of a vigilant teacher, kids feel confident, comfortable and secure."

Time to Be Unobtrusively Vigilant

Under the watch of a vigilant teacher. Students often express amazement that their teacher appears to have eyes in the back of her head. Yet the same can be said of students. Just watch when a teacher enters the high school cafeteria. Check out what happens when a teacher enters the library to pick up her class of 2nd graders. In no time, students sense (and communicate to each other) the presence of a teacher. Yet Adrienne is referring to the stability that comes when a classroom feels secure under a teacher's recognized observation. Teachers need time to look up from grading, prepping, emailing, and form-filling. The most important part of the job is literally right in front of the teacher.

Developmental psychologist William Crain discusses what Maria Montessori called "the unobtrusive presence." Crain writes, "A young child...can only

Adrienne Agena

learn freely and independently if our presence is unobtrusive." "Montessori," Crain continues, "described…ways in which sensitive parents [one could substitute 'teacher' or any protective adult here] accompany their children on walks. Such [teachers] do not force the child to keep with them, or pick them up and put them in strollers if they can't keep up. Instead, [teachers] follow the child's pace."[56]

Living in London and benefitting from many walks in the Royal Parks has given me many opportunities to see the "unobtrusive presence" in action. I often see children far away from their parents, who are watching them, yet not alongside or ahead of them. The parents are not leading the way or focusing the child's attention toward what they deem important. They are quiet and physically distant. Yet the child, sometimes humming to herself, clearly in her own world, is at peace and secure.

Adrienne Agena agrees, stating, "Students who have time to explore and make learning dynamic are comfortable in their space, confident to take risks, and willing to tackle new things with greater curiosity."

Comfortable, confident, willing to tackle. May all of our students employ those three traits as they set off on their school days. As mentioned above, comfort is generated through stability and security. Teachers bestow this upon their students, and they do this through being vigilant. Confidence, as opposed to arrogance, comes from a spirit within the student. As the offshoot of challenge and obstacles surmounted, confidence cannot be placed upon a student. It is not an externally created characteristic.

A teacher plays a huge role in building confidence in students. This confidence is strengthened when a student trusts a teacher to believe in him. The willingness to tackle the school day requires energy and a sure

> Teachers are in the perfect position to encourage their students to question broadly and brainstorm in the blue skies of the relational classroom.

sense of agency. When students are primed to go, they possess both of these elements. They are engaged in their work, they believe they have the skills (grit, especially) to succeed in doing the work, and they feel a broad classroom environment in which to test new ideas, try out new hypotheses, and expand their imagination.

Children need time to reflect and explore on their own. Teachers are

56 Crain, William (2004), *Reclaiming Childhood* (New York: Holt Paperbacks), p.28

in the perfect position to encourage their students to question broadly and brainstorm in the blue skies of the relational classroom.

Time to Have a Creative Conversation

Dr. Nancy Carlsson-Paige is an early childhood development expert and a Professor Emerita of Education at Lesley University in Cambridge, Massachusetts. She is also the founder of the University's Center for Peaceable Schools, and a founding member of Defending the Early Years, a non-profit that commissions research about early childhood education and advocates for reasoned policies for young children. She has written books and published articles about childhood, including the need to encourage exploration in learning.

I met with Nancy for lunch in Cambridge, MA, for a lively and deeply provocative discussion on the importance of play-based exploration and its key role in the development of a child's education. I had just arrived fresh from visiting Finnish school educators, and I was overdosing on Pasi Sahlberg readings, teacher-centered school environments, and residual energy from the midnight sun. As we began talking, Nancy launched directly into the main topic on her mind, one of her champion causes: that the reduction of critically important exploration time has negatively impacted early childhood learning.

"Across the nation, kindergartens have less play, less child choice, more teacher-directed activity, less arts, less music, less activity centers, and these changes are most pronounced in low-income communities of color. So what you have there is the empirical evidence that their learning is being squandered." Nancy is referring to generally-held beliefs that in low-income communities, playtime is being squeezed out for more desk time. These students are in classrooms where test preparation has become the central most important element of schooling. It is their scores on standardized tests that are viewed as most important toward judging teacher and school efficacy.

This diminishment of playtime results in stifled little brains unable to freely and deeply learn. As Nancy explains, learning is a cognitive, emotional, and physical action. "Students have to move. Through movement, they use their senses. They use their bodies, their minds, their feelings. The more they lose themselves in exploratory play, the more they are going to learn. Through neuroscience, we've gained understanding about how the brain – its synapses and neurons – fuse together in response to all this activity and engagement."

Nancy corroborates the work of Mary Helen Immordino-Yang and Mariele

M. Hardiman when she explains that holistic experiences grow neural connectivity. She uses this current research in order to challenge today's current testing-focused model of education. Preschool and elementary school students are too young to sit as often as they do at their desks and fill in bubbles on prescriptive assessments aimed at measuring rote learning. Expert teachers know this, and they find themselves torn between what they believe to be better for learning and development, and hitting benchmarks required by the state.

"Students sitting at their desks, passively, and just spitting back what's on the card that's being held up is using a really limited part of the learning capability of a child. A lot of the capacities that we need as humans, children are really developing through their active play experiences when they're little. So what is the role of the relational teacher in an exploration-based classroom? Are they paying attention to the students at play or leaving them to their own devices? What can teachers glean by observing students at play?

Good teachers are watching. They see what their students are working on and they build on it.

"Good teachers are watching. They see what their students are working on and they build on it. For example, upon completing a building project using random household objects, a group of proud students say to the teacher, 'Look how tall our building is!' The expert teacher aims to expand their learning by asking questions like, 'Well, how tall is it? How do we know how tall? How would you tell?' You used five paper towel rolls...what if we used these wooden cubes instead? How many of those would it take to make a building as high as the one you just made using paper towel rolls?' Then you're right into your math lesson.

"The relational teacher knows his or her kids well enough to know when and how to make suggestions, when and how to effectively intervene. Teaching is absolutely an art and a science."

While students are engaged in playtime, strong teachers observe and intervene when there are opportunities to build, support, and encourage. There is no 'off-duty' time for teachers, as this example shows. As the adults who supervise, educate, assess, and care for the students in their charge, teachers are not cut a break during the school day. Quite the opposite, actually. As Nancy explains, an essential part of a teacher's day is spent observing students while they are at work, play, or just resting. Yet they must account for the individual progress of each student, and deliver on write-ups, case reports, and conferences with parents several times a year.

Yet equally important is their shared observation that students are receiving less and less time for exploratory play. They are not allotted time to pretend-play, parallel-play, or role-play as they would have been a generation ago. A lot of play today is quite prescriptive, focused on 'correct' imitation rather than 'creative' imagination.

Nancy describes the difference, "Jean Piaget described play as a process where children take reality and work on it in their own way – they fit reality to their own inner understanding and needs…" In this way, Nancy points out, children take ownership of their imaginative reality. They have agency and autonomy. They are fully part of their imaginary world, and the relational teacher is not holding a magnifying glass to it, highlighting what is "wrong" about their creative exploration.

"Piaget contrasted this kind of play with imitation, which he called the opposite of play. Imitation, he said, involves mainly fitting oneself into reality. When a child imitates something, he tries to conform to some external model he has seen, as, for example, when a child acts out a wrestling move he's seen on TV." Nancy thinks there is "a bit of imitation in every child's play." However, she adds, "The *real* value of play comes about not when children directly copy an external model, but when they instead begin to bring in elements from their own experience and imagination." Seeing that one of her sons is an Oscar-winning film actor, producer and writer, Nancy has living proof of the positive impact of growing up in environments that encourage open-ended exploration through creativity.

> The real value of play comes about not when children directly copy an external model, but when they instead begin to bring in elements from their own experience and imagination.

When teachers are encouraged to encourage this in their students, the classroom is optimized. Amazing learning takes place when students are given permission to explore with blinders completely off. They are appreciated for their observations and insights. Teachers who understand that their role is to observe and build upon, rather than critique and remove, healthily enable them.

Nancy sums it up by saying, "Every idea that you have, and that I have, we invented in our own bright minds. It's not because someone told it to us and we memorized what they said. It's because we made the idea ours."

Time is required for teachers to recognize and build upon students' creative exploration. It is essential for truly connecting with students in a healthy and relational way. Those teachers who are given time to do this tend to thrive in their careers. Creativity and a joyous spirit of inquiry infuses their teaching, and as a result, students are bolstered in their learning.

Nancy and I spoke a great deal about the importance of asking the right questions as students explore topics at deeper levels. We agreed that the focus on preparing students for standardized tests has an anesthetizing effect on student curiosity. Students aren't going to ask questions when questions are being asked in a linear manner. Multiple choice. True-false. Short-answer based on regurgitation. Memorization-based response. "These students are not questioning anything. They're not questioning the statement you just made as a teacher; they're just doing what you tell them. They're getting drilled on the things the teacher's defined as learning. They're drilling it and that's basically the experience. All these other things we're seeing that really inspire education they're not experiencing. Instead, they're learning something very scary about what it means to be a citizen of the world. You obey other people.

"It seems to me that the most important things all the way through a child's schooling are two things. You help kids discover a sense of their own competence. That is, *I am a capable-thinking, problem-solving, and inventing person. I am smart, and capable, and competent.* That competence evolves socially (with others), and cognitively, and in every experiential way. Second is to instill a love of learning. Like, *I just love this, it's so much fun, it's interesting, I feel joy when I do it, I feel good about myself."*

Fourth grade teacher Meghan Elizabeth shares a story from her first year teaching in Finland. "Something that really blew me away when I came here was the first time I got negative feedback from my principal. She said, 'What you're doing is great, but these kids are just kindergarteners. Why are they already reading? The parents don't want that. They want you to build their imagination. They need to play. They need to grow. This is the most important time for them to explore. They have a long school career coming up. This is the time to teach them what they love about school. To find what they love. To establish this connection of joy of learning at school. That's great that you're doing the phonics and sound blends, but the parents don't want them reading adult newspapers and getting these other ideas in their heads. They want them to develop their imagination as much as possible. They'll learn to read next year in 1st grade. Don't push it. Maybe even 2nd grade. They don't have to be reading by the end of 1st grade.'

"This was huge. I could not imagine parents in the United States giving me that kind of feedback. It would have been the opposite. In the States, early elementary teachers have this pressure of, 'Are they reading? How is their numeracy? How are those skills? Are they able to do basic reading, writing, and math numeracy skills?' By October when you have parent conferences, I had to show off how much have I crammed into this child."

Imagine the effect the Finnish perspective has on teachers, and its impact on students. My hunch tells me Meghan's students benefitted in the long run from this exploratory (and more relaxed) approach to teaching. In conclusion, Nancy left me with the following concept to chew on as I drove through the always-jammed traffic on Mass Ave heading into Boston from Cambridge.

> ## Teaching focused on providing positive experiences and positive relationships to learning seems to me the most important thing we give students.

"Teaching focused on providing positive experiences and positive relationships to learning seems to me the most important thing we give students. This is because when they leave we want them to keep learning and to learn all their lives. We want them to turn on TED Talks. We want them to read books. We want them to be citizens, active citizens who contribute to, we hope, a healthy society. You have to do it through experience. You have to provide experiences that allow young children – students – to discover that learning is limitless, and that it's exciting, and that it's fun, and that it's thrilling."

Time to Question

I always viewed the classroom as a giant pottery wheel, at which a question is lobbed (typically by the teacher but also from students, from whom a generous amount of pulling was at times required!). The question sits there, levitating, in the middle of the room, as students sharpen their question-based instruments and shape the lump of clay into something more defined. With enough time, the answer would reveal itself, in all its iterations. This collaborative process would lead to an immense satisfaction that can only be derived from the shared experience of shaping through sculpting.

The temptation to introduce a scripted, prepackaged question is greater when time is limited. Yet the resulting feeling is a very different one – more two-dimensional, less adventurous, and certainly less motivating. Lessons that afford time to imagine and explore result in deeper retention and stronger student engagement.

Burlington High School history teacher Todd Whitten believes success in the classroom hinges on the exploratory questions he asks. He also knows that asking questions of high school students brings about close connection, even when they don't appear to care or to want to engage. In other words, sometimes a teacher needs to force an entry into a teenager's inward or guarded world to make positive gains.

"Asking questions seems to be a rarity in schools. Students go through the entire day and rarely does anyone call them by name. Nobody says, 'Nat, what do you think about that?' Teachers just point and say, 'Yes.' Or, 'Go ahead.' It's depressing.

"This idea of 'mastery objectives,' where if I all of a sudden walk up to you in a cafe and go, 'Okay, Nat, give me all 50 states and their capitals...*Go.*' If you can't, have I somehow failed? No. Have you? Technically, yes, but in the real scheme of important learning, the fault lies in the question being asked. If, on

> ## Students go through the entire day and rarely does anyone call them by name.

the other hand, I meet you at the café, sit down, and talk with you about, 'Let's plan a road trip across the country. Where do you want to go? Do you want to do northern tier, southern tier? Do you want to do this zigzag thing? Okay, let's plan that.'"

In this example, Todd demonstrates the power of exploration-based, engaging questioning. You know there are states. You know there's a country. You know there's an east and west. There are topography and weather conditions. You learn how they all interrelate in ways that engage you in your learning. The exploration that takes place leads to retention because, lo and behold, you care about the topic. It's fun, it's open-ended with possibility, and it's multidimensional.

"So I think that if we, as teachers, step away from this notion of, my job is to make you *master* something, we are better off. I think we get a much better environment for actual learning, and we get a much richer conversation between human beings. Not just between me, the holder of knowledge, and you, the empty vessel that I need to dump it in somehow."

Dr. Robin Berman, a renowned therapist and author based in Los Angeles, California, nods affirmatively when discussing the importance of teachers asking the right questions. She feels the key to excellent relational teaching lies in creating a classroom in which students understand it is *safe* to ask questions. Expert teachers know students who ask questions are not students who just "don't get it." In fact, their questions are the "build-upons" of the topic at-hand. I have found that often there is no connection between a student's comprehension of a topic and the number of questions the student asks.

Questions are clarifying (i.e., "On a trip to Mars, how does the astronaut go to the bathroom?"). In a classroom where safety is not established, students and the teacher default to thinking, *Uh-oh, that student is being rude, isn't he?* But in a safe classroom, in which a teacher has been given the time to establish classroom norms and expectations, that student's question would be approached with an open, forward-thinking mindset.

The safe classroom doesn't communicate the message that questions are used as weapons to insult or embarrass members of the classroom, including the teacher.

A teacher needs time to reflect on the origin of that question before responding. *We just discussed that it will take two years to get there; we discussed how the voyage is made in a tiny little spacecraft; we saw samples of astronaut food from the Space Age. His question was generated from the space of curiosity, not malice.* In a safe classroom where questions are used to shape the topic being discussed (in this case, the possibility of travel to Mars), questions are assets. The safe classroom doesn't communicate the message that questions are used as weapons to insult or embarrass members of the classroom, including the teacher.

How does a teacher allow for open questioning? Robin explains, "At the core, teaching is an emotional relationship. Are teachers taught about the power of words, shaming ones versus inspiring ones? Are they taught how their facial expressions talk, do they roll their eyes and look exasperated?"

The students are watching. A teacher who responds to student questions with defensive body language, a closed mindset, dismissive sighs, and eye-rolls can have a damaging impact on a student excited about exploring and discovering answers that will provide a clearer lens with which to view the world.

One of the most valuable lessons students can receive in school is the strength to ask questions without hesitation, nervousness, or anxiety. While children are not delicate special snowflakes constantly at risk of melting with every bit of negative feedback, they are easily defeated when they sense impatience and dismissiveness from the only adult in the room. When this happens, it's easy for trust to be broken. The extra demands being put on teachers today add to the struggle of maintaining a sense of calmness, warmth and openness.

This must change. As Robin so eloquently states, "You have to be mindful when you're holding someone's soul." As the adult with the second-most influential role in a growing child's life, this fact demands that teachers draw from their emotional reserves each and every day. They are indeed holders of souls. We teach to souls, but we reveal our own in the process. The vulnerability of being a child or young adult unquestionably exists in every student, from kindergarten through senior year. Teachers have the power to nurture and affirm the dreams of children. Yet, as history teacher Colleen Kyle stated in an earlier chapter, they also have the power to trample on and destroy them.

Time is the essential component for facilitating a benevolent approach essential to teaching souls. It's not an issue of "teaching minutes" and "rocks in the stream" when discussing optimal school schedules. It's primarily about allowing for time for connection, serendipity, and grace that can be generated only in classrooms made safe to explore through open, active, and brave questioning.

Robin shared an amazing story. "While I was studying for my medical school entrance exams, I was teaching kindergarten, and this little boy stood on a book. He had dropped the book and was just standing on it. My first reaction was to correct, 'We don't stand on books.' But instead, I decided to connect. I asked, 'Sam, why are you standing on that book?' I asked this question in a gentle tone, not a harsh, punitive one. His answer: 'I want to go *in*.'"

> Teachers have the power to shut you down or open you up.

A moment of silence spread across us as I processed the five-year-old's response, while recognizing that not in a million years would I have imagined it. As if reading my mind, Robin noted, "Teachers have the power to shut you down or open you up."

The wisdom of children from the mouths of babes. This young boy probably knew he was in a precarious position, and he was perhaps steeling himself for a confrontation. Yet because Robin asked him an open, non-judgmental question, he was able to safely respond with his beautiful answer. With those words, this boy brought her back to being a kindergartener. The wonder, the imagination, the sense of possibility that so bitterly seeps out of our system as we age.

In Robin, this boy found a kindred spirit who enjoyed his sense of curiosity instead of thinking, "I'm going to teach this boy how to follow rules. We don't stand on books in kindergarten." Robin cared to know what he was thinking as he stood on the book. As she puts it, "You don't have access to a child's truth if you have judgment."

The relationship between exploration and wonder is deep. Even today, when I think about exploration, I envision examples from my past. I think about walking the path between my and my friend's house under a full moon. I recall digging along the riverside for arrowheads, using the evidence to round out my understanding of a past civilization. I also recall looking through the telescope at the Wellesley College Observatory and seeing craters on the moon with such detail that it felt like I was tracing my fingers along the bumps, crevasses, and lunar sea beds. In these instances, I envisioned myself there – walking the path under branches illuminated by the moon, in the Wampanoag riverside village, or on the moon touching its cold, rocky, powdery surface.

As exploration expands wonder in the classroom, students open their eyes, and seemingly their minds, wider. Wonder is the bread swelling in the oven. Curiosity is the thickening agent. Exploration is the heat that makes the dough rise. The classroom is the kitchen. The teacher is the chef de cuisine. The students are the assistant chefs (perhaps a few are sous chefs, managing the others). The ingredients are found within the textbooks, computers, and other sources of information. The recipe is contained within the teacher-generated prompts.

I once had a parent compliment my teaching by sharing the impact of what I thought was a simple lesson – reading aloud. As the Assistant Headmaster at an independent school in Los Angeles, California, I read to each 4th grade class once a week. One year, I read *Journey to the Center of the Earth* by Jules Verne; the next year, I chose a different book. Reading to them was a way for me to get to know each student not just as a transcript, but as an individual with a unique personality. We'd head outside. The students would sit or lie down under a tree, with eyes open or closed, while I sat in a chair. I interrupted my reading with frequent questions to refocus the drifting students, allowing them to share thoughts in a wide open but secure space.

The parent explained, "My son told me, 'I could *hear* it. I could *hear* the book without pressure to perform, I could just enjoy learning.' Clearly, what my son got from lying on his back outside of the classroom under that tree and listening to you read was deep. Then he was inspired to go to the library that afternoon to finish the book on his own initiative, not for a test. Just for the sheer joy of learning. I just love the image of my son lying under a tree – open, no crunching over the desk." To me, these reading experiences combined the physical, environmental, and intellectual in a way that encouraged exploration and deep engagement.

Steven ("Steve") Chan has spent 25 years in the classroom. Steve is currently the middle school director at Laguna Blanca School in Santa Barbara, California, where he still teaches a section of world history to his fortunate students. Introverted and reflective yet armed with a wickedly dry sense of humor and a clear love for both history and school communities, Steve is a true educational leader. In our interview, Steve echoed the abovementioned parent's strong belief in the soulful value of exploration, particularly as it intersects with building character. "I look at my role as broadening perspectives through exploration. I want them to think about everything that's out there. I want them to think about all the perspectives that are out there, and to come to their own conclusions, and to be open-minded enough to allow for a change of opinion that they might not necessarily have seen or noticed or cared about before."

As Dr. Robin Berman notes, "When you feel seen and known by a teacher, you open up emotional channels. Teaching is a heart and soul process. If you don't feel safe with a parent, you can't connect. If you don't feel safe with a teacher, you can't really learn." She continues, "Great teachers are remembered most for how they made a child feel."

Teachers need time to encourage exploration and wonderment. Teaching is a spiritual endeavor, and the image of one's "soul com(ing) out" through learning with a relational teacher in a safe environment is the perfect image of expert, optimal teaching. The end result might or might not be a perfectly risen loaf of bread, but the process is guaranteed to be rewarding in and of itself.

Teaching is a heart and soul process. If you don't feel safe with a parent, you can't connect. If you don't feel safe with a teacher, you can't really learn.

We live in a techno-centric age where science, technology, engineering, math, and facts are king. Still, an optimal classroom remains a space that allows for wonderment and imagination. Our future depends on this because pioneer thinkers have all been daydreamers, questioners, and creative thinkers who pondered, "What if?" In his harrowing yet important book, *Glow Kids*, Nicholas Kardaras addresses concerns that rise when wonderment is at odds with today's science-based, answer-focused society. "Science has stripped us of our myths, telling us that there are no gods or demons, no heaven and hell, no Elysian mysteries, no Santa Claus and no tooth fairy. Indeed, we are told by science that the world is a rather cold, mechanistic place without myth or meaning – the necessary life blood of the human psyche."[57] Teachers need time to promote exploration so the classroom can remain an incubator for ideas that grow from unbridled imagination.

Time to Improvise

Another lens to use while looking at the valuable use of exploration in the classroom involves the craft of improvisation. Shortly after moving to Los Angeles, I tried out improvisation as a way to stretch myself and meet new people. In Los Angeles, improvisation ("improv") workshops can be found in every neighborhood. I took my introductory class at Second City in Hollywood (Why not go big out of the gate?). My outlook literally switched during the first hour of my first class. Through Second City, I learned that improvisation is not merely an acting technique, but also a way to view the personal interactions that occur throughout life. "It's not about yes, but…" when responding to a question. "It's yes, and…" When a student asks a question that seems obtuse, or responds to a question with an answer that seems from left field, a teacher is required to respond – and that response has an impact on the classroom dynamic.

> The word 'but' can undermine and undo all the positive feedback you've given yourself in the first half of the sentence, while the word 'and' helps you notice that you've actually got two, separable thoughts there: one about what worked, and a second one about what more you could do.

Educator Stephen Wangh explains that the word "but" stunts intellectual growth in the classroom and the word "and" facilitates growth. "The word 'but' can undermine and undo all the positive feedback you've given yourself in the first half of the sentence, while the word 'and' helps you notice that you've actually got two, separable thoughts there: one about what worked, and a second one about what more you could do."[58]

For example, when a student answers in a manner that the teacher thinks is extraordinarily off-base, the teacher faces a choice. He could acknowledge

---

57 Kardaras, Nicholas (2016), *Glow Kids* (New York: St. Martin's Press), p.12
58 Wangh, Stephen (2013), *The Heart of Teaching* (New York: Routledge Press), p.47

the student's response (sometimes it helps to repeat what the student said to reassure that he was heard) with a simple, "Yes." That word is affirmative at its base level. In the classroom, it means, "I hear you." It also states, "Your input is openly received." It also connotes a positive approach. Even if the student contributed the utterly incorrect response, the teacher is acknowledging the effort and risk of a class contribution. If using an improvisation approach, "yes" would be followed up by "yes, and… ."

In contrast, the "no" response offers a choice: we can either explore together how the student arrived at the incorrect answer, or call on another student who, as a salvation-in-waiting, will give the correct answer and clean up the former student's mess.

"No" is not wrong. In a right/wrong class like math, in particular, it is a perfectly acceptable (and, I'd argue, important) response to give. Yet how is it followed up? Can we take the "no" answer, and use it as a springboard to get to "yes"? Are we letting it go, permitting it to fly around the classroom like a satellite out of orbit? Are we using it as an opening to guide the class through the order of operations that led to this incorrect answer? These approaches require time. They also require a level of pre-established trust in the classroom. Finally, they require a student to feel recognized for the value of his input, even if incorrect, as long as the student has offered sincere input. Since the essence of exploration views classroom cultures as being shaped through positive mindsets, time invested in these approaches can be time well spent. However, if the opposite is true – if a student is taking the opportunity to be clearly defiant, mocking, and thus rude, the teacher response requires something different – and direct.

Interestingly, the "yes" response can also be a conversation stopper – unless it is followed up with a new opener. For example, The Archer School English teacher Jen Dohr explains, "When kids say, 'I agree' (i.e., 'yes'), what they're really saying is, 'the point is done.' I've agreed with Gabby, so my job is finished. When they say, 'I disagree' (i.e., 'no'), the same thing happens: that point is done. Both responses fail to see the layers, the dimensions of a discussion. So I teach my students to respond, 'I hear you, and I think…' to one another. So they're building an interpersonal connection as they're deepening their critical thinking skills."

I recalled to Jen a memory of teachers who responded to me as a student with, "I disagree with you" and how I would immediately become defensive and feel shut down. I reflected with her about how much more effective it would have been if they'd responded instead with, "I hear you, and I'm going to actually go in a little bit of a different direction, but I did hear you.'"

Jen continues, "I think modeling this language is so important. When a student's point isn't ripe, I constantly feather in statements like, 'I hear you. I'm still chewing on that. It's not resonating with me yet.' That 'yet' is so important because you are not closing the door; you are affirming a growth mindset. 'I want to keep thinking about what you said,' and 'I'm coming back to you, I want to see what you're seeing' are perhaps the most powerful messages of self-worth a student can hear."

Parker Palmer highlights the role of "yes-and" when he writes, "Niels Bohr...offers the keystone I want to build on: 'The opposite of a true statement is a false statement, but the opposite of a profound truth can be another profound truth.' In certain circumstances, truth is found not by splitting the world into either-ors, but by embracing it as *both-and*."[59] Here, Parker perfectly sums up the importance of incorporating "both-and" in order to shape a classroom environment that allows for the grey complexities of truth versus falsehood, right versus wrong.

An improvisation-based approach not only facilitates deeper classroom dialogue. It is also a key element toward embracing possibility and recognizing capabilities in the classroom. Ms. Ann Diederich is a 20-year world language teacher at Polytechnic School in Pasadena, California. Armed with a passionate love for language and culture, Ann models the Rassias method in her language classes. While never literally throwing out the textbook, Ann allocates healthy portions of her class period to group games, acting exercises, and culturally relevant and topical lessons. Students are infused by Ann's creativity and passion. In this way, one watches Chip Williams' "light my lamp from your lamp" in vivid tableau. Ann states, "I'm constantly striving for students to be open to possibilities. Improvisation activities build a community...it's *primordial*: it's about setting the stage. And when it works, it's magical. I've got kids getting up and dancing...I couldn't ask for more." Getting high school kids to get up and dance in language class takes some extraordinary talent. Yet it's not impossible! If the teacher communicates an openness toward expression, and a positive approach to student input, the sky is indeed the limit. This requires tapping into the "primordial" in all of us.

Our base elements...the components that make us feel alive and human.

> ## Improvisation activities build a community...it's primordial: it's about setting the stage. And when it works, it's magical.

59   Palmer, Parker (1998), *The Courage to Teach* (San Francisco: Jossey-Bass), p.64

Ann Diederich

The image this conjures from me is from the play *The History Boys* by Alan Bennett, in which so much of the action takes place in a living, dynamic, creative-filled history classroom (which includes an upright piano that is used often by the students during spontaneous outbursts of improvisation, both related to and unrelated to the topic being studied).

Improvisation techniques are effective tools toward establishing positive behavior in the classroom. Meghan Elizabeth, the 4th grade teacher from Helsinki, discussed how improvisation techniques work in establishing behavioral codes in her classrooms. "It's not the teacher saying, 'You have to be like this.' Instead, it involves asking, 'What do you think a fair, balanced way would be to behave in this situation?' Then they have a discussion about it. They might act it out. They might role-play, 'Oh, he broke my phone while he was using it. Now he just gave it back to me broken, and didn't say sorry, and doesn't want to pay for it. What do we do?' I have found that my students love role-playing. They love to explore through improvisation. They love it."

Clearly, exploration transcends the academic in the classroom. Relational teachers understand this to be true in myriad dimensions: learning for knowledge, cultivating character, and embracing the strengths of risk-taking. As a tool for exploration, improvisation strengthens the relational connection between teacher and student. It shapes dialogue, impacts behavior, expands possibility and encourages optimism. Improvisation is truly an example of the capabilities of the human spirit.

Time to Light the Lamp

Elizabeth ("Liz") Ganem personifies the compassionate, fired-up, insightful middle school teacher we hope our children have at least once in their lives. Liz teaches at The Willows Community School in Culver City, CA, and has been teaching for just over 20 years. Even today, she maintains the same youthful energy and vigor she had when I first met her in 1997 in graduate school at Middlebury College in Middlebury, Vermont. At that time, we were adversaries on the ultimate frisbee field, where I would often choose to cover her because she was such a fun challenge. Liz has the strength to tackle anything – not just physically, but emotionally as well. Her heart is open to friends, students, even strangers in need. Her joy for teaching results in classrooms made safe for exploration.

Liz and I met on the back patio of a Santa Monica coffeehouse on an overcast day in midwinter. Decked out in a North Face puffy jacket and sunglasses, her spirit lit up an otherwise dreary late afternoon.

> The act of teachers noticing students can produce motivation in students because they know they're not being formally observed and evaluated, but clearly and plainly seen.

The unpredictability of students not only keeps Liz on her feet, but also fuels her enthusiasm for teaching. I can relate to this, as it's the colorful human elements of the school community that remind us we house evolving, messy human beings as opposed to suited-up, corporate adults.

We opened our discussion about the importance of time for exploration with a recent experience Liz had with a massive lamp-building project. Over 70 students signed up to spend a week building lamps. None of them – the 10 supervising teachers included – had any background in lamp-building. Yet this experience stands out as an example of the power of exploration, of not-knowing and how shared inquiry can bring a school community closer together through the shared pursuit of an intrinsically motivated project.

"I wish you could've seen these kids. They would plug in their lamps and they'd light up themselves. 'It works! Look! It works. Come see my lamp!' Normally, when my students are working, I'll walk around and ask them questions. For example, during this project, I would ask how a student is doing, and he or she might say, 'I used the hand drill on this piece of wood and it took me all day. But I did it, I made a hole and now I'm on to the next step.'"

This example implies that it's not so much the content of a teacher's feedback that's important; what's most important is the idea of kids being *noticed*. The act of teachers noticing students can produce motivation in students because they know they're not being formally observed and evaluated, but clearly and plainly *seen*. This can reinforce a student's motivation and fuel the fire for further work. The lesson is that sometimes teachers can feel pressure to give 'meaningful' feedback (i.e., drive the car), when all a student really needs to move forward is to be commented on, even with blithe detachment. Of course, with adolescents in particular, too much attention can produce the opposite effect – the turtle retreating into her shell.

Liz clearly intuits the importance of allowing her students to have agency and ownership over their work. Ownership tends to produce feelings of pride in one's work, and both ownership and pride are key elements of the flow-state.

What about students who don't feel pride in their work? How about students who need support, not praise? How does a teacher fuel their drive to explore? Is a teacher sometimes not the right person for this – perhaps someone else can do a better job, with the teacher shuffling out of the way?

"For some students, the wind quickly goes out of their sails if they aren't getting where they perceive they should be. For example, this girl hadn't finished her lamp. She wanted to make it look like a tree, but she couldn't get the branches to attach the way she'd envisioned. Instead of being resilient, she initially said to me, 'I give up. I'm done.' So I tried to support her. 'All right, let's try to figure this out.' When she saw me moving the branches around, I

> The ability to resist the temptation to coddle and instead let go develops as a teacher becomes more expert.

suggested, 'If we can get these two up like that...' But she wasn't interested.

"Moments later, an older 8th grader came by and said, 'You don't need all four of the branches up, because some branches on trees go down, too.' She responded. 'You're right.' After the 8th grader's suggestion, she could see how to achieve the goal she'd set for herself. She developed a sense of ownership by tweaking the outcome based on the student's suggestion."

In teaching, the messenger matters. Liz was astute enough to see that the 8th grader had more pull on the 6th grader in this instance. She allowed him to make his suggestion (which the student followed, most likely influenced by the attention given by an older student she admired). Instead of leaving it at that, however, Liz returned to affirm what had just happened. She didn't affirm that the student followed her advice; rather, she affirmed what she witnessed as the student displaying ownership over her project. The 8th grader's feedback was a vital catalyst for the 6th grade student, and Liz knew to back away and allow for the peer support to take place. The ability to resist the temptation to coddle and instead let go develops as a teacher becomes more expert. The notion of leading from behind the curtain becomes fully understood.

Andrea Archer, a career educator from Wales, UK, taught science for years before moving into administration and becoming the Head of School at three excellent independent schools in the United States. When reflecting upon her teaching years, Andrea immediately brings up the importance of exploration in her science classes. Like Liz, Andrea created a science classroom that was project-based and rooted in shared inquiry. Also like Liz, Andrea supported the value of testing hypotheses and allowing them to fail. As a science teacher, Andrea was highly regarded for her ability to engage students through building a supportive student–teacher relationship.

"One of the first things that passionate science teachers learn is the need to demystify science and the belief that it is fundamentally too challenging or too focused on memorizing a vast body of facts. True exploration in the classroom or research laboratory takes a commitment of time, patience and a willingness to validate creative thinking that may lead to numerous dead ends. Giving kids the freedom to direct their own learning can certainly cause confusion and frustration in the classroom but the resulting depth of understanding and ownership is well worth the effort."

In this comment, Andrea cites ownership of one's efforts as a prime reward for "true exploration". By "ownership", Andrea implies "agency". As a teacher of adolescents, Andrea focused her relational teaching skills on bolstering student agency – of hypotheses and experiments – so that the end result will not only be a factual answer but also stronger self-esteem. Also in this response, Andrea acknowledges what we have addressed several times so far in this book: learning is messy. As she notes, getting to the answer involves a circuitous path that becomes clear only in hindsight. This was visually reinforced in her classroom, which had a quote from Albert Einstein on the wall: *"Anyone who has never made a mistake has never tried anything new."*

In our interview, Andrea described to me one of her favorite science projects, which is a fourth grade experiment that tests the absorbency and wet strength of multiple brands of paper towels. Students are instructed to determine which brand gives the best value for money, and the answer often contradicts what they've been led to believe by advertisers.

Andrea states, "Some students launch into their trials with great enthusiasm while others will try everything in their power to get me to reveal 'the right approach'. I have learned over the years that my instinct to rescue my students from failure is strong and something that I need to resist and allow poorly constructed ideas to run their course. Instead of focusing on outcomes I put all my energy into helping students navigate their group dynamics as they strive to incorporate myriad ideas through brainstorming and negotiation to agree on an experimental design and divide the tasks during experimentation."

I love what Andrea is speaking of here, because she addresses what teachers (and parents) feel when they leave their students to their own devices. When the inevitable mistake comes along, a teacher's corrective instinct is extremely strong and thus hard to resist. Yet the value is exponential if a teacher resists the temptation to course-correct for the students rather than having the students do this for themselves.

> My instinct to rescue my students from failure is strong and something that I need to resist

On the concept of failing greatly while exploring, Andrea states that "False starts, failures and unexpected successes are all part of the learning process and the animated conversations about experimental controls and the need for accurate measurements are as important as answering the question, 'which paper towel should your parents buy and why?' The benefits that we gain from supporting each group's design, regardless of the flaws, teaches far more than science and helps students embrace future exploration and risk-taking in the classroom." These benefits fall into the category of life skills. Supporting each other, taking risks, trying over again and again are all skills that Andrea's science classes developed. These skills far outlasted the academic year and presumably live in her students in their adult lives today.

Time to Honor the Adult-Child-Adult

When looking back on her life, the lamp-building English teacher Liz Ganem remembers, "I didn't want to feel coddled in high school, but I definitely wanted to be noticed as a person and as a writer. The ability to notice is important as a teacher. Just trying to imagine what the students are thinking, or trying to have some empathy for where they're coming from. It takes patience, understanding, and a lot of love. These middle school students are going through so much. They feel like, *I'm an adult. Wait, I'm a child. I'm an adult. I'm a child.*" At that age, both self-concepts are true. For teachers of middle school students, time is needed to be able to recognize, acknowledge, and affirm both sides, knowing that the adult side will ultimately win out as the student grows.

Liz mentions a teacher who made a strong impression on her through his ability to observe both sides with empathy. "My 8th grade English teacher, Mr. Hopkins, noticed me. One day, after a heated class, he was on lunch duty. He walked by me and said, 'Nice work on *The Naked and the Nude* today. That's a tough poem to tackle and you did it very well." We had just debated that Robert Graves poem earlier that day. I had said something in class that indicated that I was really fired up about this poem. I don't recall what I'd said in that class, but I do recall feeling deeply invested in the discussion.

"Mr. Hopkins remembered what I'd said. At that moment, I felt like I had a voice. What I feel about the moment was powerful. He wanted to let me know that I spoke, and he heard me. And he remembered it hours later. That was it. That was a turning point for me in my self-concept as an emerging writer."

At that moment, I felt like I had a voice. What I feel about the moment was powerful.

Mr. Hopkins could see the emerging adult in 8th grade Liz. By merely mentioning the title of the poem that had fired her up, he communicated that she had made a memory for him. She was heard and seen and remembered and affirmed. Thirty-plus years later, Liz still remembers the impact he had on her. Liz now replicates the power of this action in interactions with her students.

"As a teacher, I love seeing when a student gets excited about a topic. Then I can make suggestions to further that interest. *Read this book. See this movie. Try this article.* There was a student I taught years ago who was deeply interested in D-Day. She would ask, 'Did you ever know about this part of it?' I would respond, 'Yes, and did you know about this?' And she would say, 'No.' She would go off and explore it on her own. I never gave her resources. At some point later that year, she wanted to start a history club, where we could talk about history at lunch. We had t-shirts made up that said, *We are Past Lovers.*"

First, how great a name is that for a history club?! Second, how powerful of a motivating force is teacher interest? Exploration, when a solo endeavor, needs fueling by positive reinforcement because the fire can extinguish itself through exhaustion, boredom, or self-defeat. Liz fueled her student's exploration by not only affirming it, but also contributing to it with suggestions for additional resources and layered questions that expanded the student's understanding of D-Day. Supporting a student's desire for exploration doesn't have to involve huge amounts of legwork; sometimes it just means making room for another to step in (the peer example from the lamp project), remembering a fiery contribution hours later (*The Naked and the Nude*), or adding more ideas and/or resources to a topic that excites the student (such as a club with a fun name).

Liz continues, "A key part of what makes a school important today (especially in this age of technology) is that it teaches us how to work with other people. How to have the ability to sit quietly with a book for longer than 20 minutes. How to listen. How to question. It's as necessary to be in that environment as a student now as it was back when I was in school.

"Maybe it's even more necessary now, because we can be so cut off from people. I'm amazed at how many times I go somewhere, and there's a group of people, and nobody's really even aware of each other, because they're all doing this (she imitates someone texting).

"School is a place where people are talking, people are listening, and everyone is interacting. School is a place to use one's imagination to explore an idea. At its core, school is a place that encompasses people who care about each other. School requires people to share the same space and work together. The teachers are working together and reinforcing the same message to their students. They are encouraging of the same things, discouraging of the same things. That's always going to be important to the meaningfulness of school."

As we wrapped up our conversation, Liz dug into the core of why we teach. "Honestly, it comes down to love. The kids love when we're silly in class, and doing stuff that's just human and honest. As their teacher, I want them to know that I really care about them. That I love my job. That I love being in the classroom. Because I do. I love that dynamism. I love that the atmosphere in the classroom is always changing. Sometimes it can be a slog, and as a teacher you find yourself trying so hard to get the students to understand the Oxford comma rule. Yet the spirit in the classroom offers up the chance that maybe at that moment a student will make a

> The core of my classroom is centered on love – for humanity in all its permutations, for the messiness of adolescents, for the concepts being taught, and the challenges and successes that result from taking risks through exploration in the safe environment of the classroom.

comment from way out in left field, and suddenly everyone will crack up, and we move on, feeling a sense of relaxation from just laughing together. Those are great moments that remind me that the core of my classroom is centered on love – for humanity in all its permutations, for the messiness of adolescents, for the concepts being taught, and the challenges and successes that result from taking risks through exploration in the safe environment of the classroom."

World language teacher Alan Rivera echoes the love that Liz so eloquently describes when he states, "when you take away the 'teacher persona' and you just be yourself and you show kids that you love this thing that you do and you want them to love it, too, they get it." He's right. Armed with authentic passion for the subject one teaches, a relational teacher is able to explore without bounds by unharnessing the love – of subject, of student, and of inquiry-based exploration.

Recapping the Relational: Enthusiastically Explore

Once the relational bridge-building has been achieved through connection and trust, a teacher can encourage exploration in the classroom. Exploration involves freedom: to be creative, to wonder, to inquire and to broaden. This broadening of the mind and the spirit is permitted through the distant yet vigilant watch of a relational teacher. It is imperative that wonderment is a central element of any K–12 classroom. "Blue-sky thinking" is a corporate term I can live with!

Schools should be designed with open spaces in their blueprints. Literal open spaces in which students can explore in nature. Symbolic open spaces of the mind where students can feel free to generate questions and explore them to completion. In both cases, the teacher is in the role of a shepherd. He is a strong figure of stability to whom the students are aware. He is also an unobtrusively vigilant teacher who leads from behind. He allows for students to speak with each other on their own level, using their own terminology, because he recognizes that expert teachers "follow the child's pace." He permits individual approaches toward tackling a well-prepared question. He is there to swoop in at a moment's notice if the student gets derailed and falls off the proper path.

Liz Ganem emulates the powerful impact of exploration in the classroom when she describes the lamp project. She reminisces on how important a teacher's curiosity is to a young, impressionable student. By holding these student memories in the forefront of her mind, Liz is able to encourage learning through exploration in her own students. When she speaks about her students, she communicates a genuine fascination toward the way her students think and how they perceive their world and themselves.

Drs. Nancy Carlsson-Paige and Robin Berman complement each other when they explain the importance of an open approach toward exploratory learning. When Nancy bemoans the diminishment of unstructured playtime in schools, she addresses a very real issue in child development. She differentiates imitation from play. There is too much structure where it shouldn't be, and this is troubling, especially when addressing young children. As Robin Berman asserts, young children need room to grow their minds and their sense of place in the world. They need encouragement to try new ideas through creating and answering open-ended questions. There are too many yes/no tests circulating in school environments. Expert teachers buck this trend as best as they can, yet quantitative measurements seem to lurk around too many school corners.

Optimal classrooms do not believe in the shut-down power of "yes" and "no." These stop-words smother the fires of enthusiasm and possibility. Relational teachers follow these two words as a master improviser would – with "and" or the like. When Nancy describes teaching as an art, she is referring to the remarkably savvy skills expert teachers utilize when drawing out conversation when a simple black or white response would be much easier to give. The students feel the effort these teachers make. When a teacher is able to communicate honest feedback with encouragement, the resulting feeling is empowerment. Exploration provides the opportunity for students to feel empowered to tackle complex questions through open inquiry and affirming interactions between themselves and their teacher.

At one point during our interviews, Burlington High School history teacher Todd Whitten reflected on the importance of autonomy in exploration. "It was just last Friday," he began. "I came home exhausted. Absolutely flatlined." Todd's beaming grin betrayed his true feelings…he was utterly happy while sharing this memory. "Yet it was the greatest feeling. It was one of those moments where I decided to toss the lesson plan and prep my tail off for the unit and incorporate all new material, approaches, and connections. I grinded on the prep-work, visualizing how it would be designed for the 'funnel effect'. And those students were funneled and the results were amazing! It was a reminder of how even a 20-year teacher can feel euphoric when a unit goes so well. Yet it wouldn't have had that depth if I hadn't been given the autonomy to plan my own lessons and tailor them toward these specific students. And I recognize the unsustainability of this…I have kids at home. I'm a department chair. I'm not in my young 20s anymore. But this is what it feels like to be a teacher and it feels amazing. And utterly exhausting!"

Todd is describing a feeling that is deeper than delivering on an assigned task. He gained through not only knowing that his students were learning complex material thanks to the way he'd structured and paced the lesson. He gained also by knowing that he communicated the lesson in accordance with the students in front of him. He knew that Mark would be interested in the social justice element of the lesson. Sybil would be fascinated by the contrarian perspective. Jordan would be excited by the research. Taylor would thrive with the collaborative element. In this way, Todd connected with his students as individuals and he wove this knowledge into a lesson plan that depleted him yet also filled him up.

Todd connected with his students as individuals and he wove this knowledge into a lesson plan that depleted him yet also filled him up.

His "cup overflowed", and he opened those floodgates to his students, who gave him much more in return through their enthusiastic exploration.

Steve Chan

Time to be hopeful

"Even though we face the difficulties of today and tomorrow, I still have a dream."

Martin Luther King, Jr.

Studies confirm that hope is an important factor in developing a classroom environment for optimal learning. Hope is wonder. Wonder is imagination. Imagination is risk-taking. Risk-taking is confidence. Teachers possess eternal hope in their students. Hope that they will do their best with their students. Hope that their efforts will be received and rewarded through student learning. Hope that what they do matters and that their impact will last beyond time shared in the classroom.

Peggy, a distraught 7th grade math teacher sits across my desk from me. It's the end of a busy week. With the school fair taking place that Spring weekend, activity has been heightened. A typical spring lament by teachers is, "I can't get anything done." Or, "I might as well just throw in the towel and close out the year now." In spring, these sorts of sentiments transcend everything – every complaint, expression of stress, even excitement over summer vacation. Meetings of this nature are typically the counterpoint to a dramatic classroom event. The teacher will be understandably emotional. I learned long ago not to prod, but to just listen. We are all therapists.

"It's Trevor. He and I had an altercation in class and…" She reaches for tissues. I slide the box over.

"He is just not working. He hasn't all year. It's like he just doesn't care about math. About me."

I want to interject, but move into the happy place I have built in my gut over the years. Yes, this beachside cabana front porch is exactly where I'll set up my hammock.

"You know what I mean? He's just not an academic. He's not a worker. I just can't believe he's going to finish the school year with just as little motivation, and care, as he started it with." She holds up her hand and flashes a "zero" sign.

We sit in silence together for what feels like a minute.

"So I pulled him aside after class and expressed it to him. He didn't even look at me! I told him that his inability to look me in the eye indicates his lack of respect for me. Well, that caused him to turn beet red. I can't tell if it was anger or embarrassment, but I told him everything he failed to do this year. He needs to know! So I told him. And you know what he did? He turned his back on me. I said 'get back here!' and he continued walking out the door. Can you believe it! He absolutely defied me. I am so mad at him!"

She didn't need to tell me she was mad. Her anger had become rage, and she was quickly becoming what she feared Trevor had become. She wiped tears from her eyes.

Finally, I spoke. "I know you've had issues with Trevor all year. I remember his parents after parent-teacher conferences. Remember they came to me about how they feared you weren't connecting with him?"

She nodded. "Thank you for defending me."

"Do you feel like you turned things around after that?"

"Nat, can I tell you something? I don't think there's any way I could motivate this young man. He just doesn't have the skills to succeed."

He doesn't have the skills to succeed.

We discussed Stanford professor Carol Dweck back in the chapter, "Time to Validate" in which we relate the use of the word "brilliant" to motivation. When Dweck's book *Mindset* was published in 2012, it caused a revolution in the world of education. Her claim is that every student can succeed if she receives proper feedback for her work – feedback centered on effort (process) over result (product). Inherent in that claim is the idea that no one is "fixed" – everyone can create new neural pathways, alter their memories, or deepen their long-term retention.

This teacher was viewing Trevor with a fixed mindset of her own – by critiquing his fixed mindset (i.e., potential) in math.

When I first read Dweck's seminal work, I experienced mixed feelings of validation and curiosity. I was validated in that my deepest instincts about students were proven correct: everyone can succeed in school. Expert teachers hold this belief as sacrosanct. I felt curiosity, however, that Dweck's approach was being hailed by so many educators as revolutionary. A growth mindset is centered on hope. It proved to me a need for the argument of hope. Unbridled, unconditional, unwavering hope is something all expert teachers possess. And the students know it. But the response to Dweck's premise indicates this doesn't come natural to some teachers, not because it is a foreign concept, but because hope takes time to cultivate – time to connect with each student, time to understand what makes each student tick, and time to express the belief that the student not only can do the work, but also excel at it.

Yet many teachers work in an environment that lacks hope – or belief – in students, parents, colleagues, administrators, and the profession as a whole. Probably no one is surprised to read this, since practically every day there seems to be a news article about a teacher accused of doing something illegal, a standardized testing failure, or a new reason why teachers are failing "our kids."

This oppressive environment worms its way into the psyche of teachers. As individual microcosms in the world of education, schools must try to negate these negative perspectives. By celebrating teaching as a calling and treating it as a profession, schools can help empower teachers to believe in their students and in teachers' power to change lives. Schools must devote time to developing hope in their faculty, and acknowledging the supreme importance of teachers having hope in their students. Schools can do this in part by celebrating the healthy relationships between teachers and students. This will help create cultures of partnership and shared achievements between teachers and students.

Hope is one of the core reasons why people choose to be teachers in the first place. Teachers are often drawn into the profession by memories of teachers who opened their own sense of hope – the kindergarten teacher who taught them to explore the colors of the rainbow or the 12th grade astronomy teacher who blew minds while discussing the origins of the universe. Hope is the dopamine of student engagement. It is inherent in literature, equations, and foreign languages, and visible in a teacher's expressions and comments.

Teachers feed on hope expressed by their students. Often when a teacher states that when he teaches he "feels younger," it's a recognition of the powerful force of hopeful idealism in his young students.

Yet hope is not regenerative on its own. To expect such would be magical thinking, as no one possesses limitless hope. To do so would require blinders thick to the social, political, and economic world. Having hope requires work. With work, hope becomes regenerative, yet not infinite. For hope to exist, one needs to acknowledge that the world can be both wondrous and heartbreaking.

A thriving school environment understands the need for hope within its community. It is central to its culture, and transcendent in every realm of the organization.

Time to Honor Hope in the Homeroom

Andy Barnett, the School Chaplain in Washington, D.C., speaks about hope and its connection to student motivation. "Hope is absolutely woven into the kids when they are successfully being pushed. They're thinking, 'My teacher believes I can do this work. If I'm prepared, I have better days in class.' There is an understanding of the value of working for something: the joy, discovery that comes with that. It's a sense of, 'we are working together – we believe in what we are doing together.'"

Henry, a 6th grade student in Los Angeles, California, emphasizes the importance of a coaching approach in the classroom. "I think the teacher should sort of be like a sports coach. If they pick you on a team, then they believe in you and they're on your side. They want you to learn. Sometimes when you're at practice and the coach pushes you, you think he's being mean but he's not. He's on your side. He's trying to push you to get you into better shape for the academics. Yes, something like that. Not as much like in a mean way, he doesn't care about your academics as much as he really cares about pushing you to your limits."

There is a lot of trust in Henry's depiction of how an expert teacher approaches the classroom. Henry connects a coach to his team. When you're on a coach's team, the coach "believe(s) in you" and is "on your side." That alignment is huge, and at the core of this strong teacher-student relationship is hope.

Henry explains that being a teacher-coach implies challenging one's teammates. It's all about "pushing." "Sometimes…you think he's being mean but he's not." When a child refers to a teacher as "mean," he could be describing a wide range of behaviors. A mean teacher could be just that

– resentful, sarcastic, shaming, etc. Yet a mean teacher also could be driven. Intense. Committed. Unwavering. As we move into the 'cooler' (i.e., less heated) definitions of "mean," we move into relational teacher territory.

In his book, *Pedagogy of the Oppressed*, Brazilian educator Paulo Freire defines hope in the classroom as fuel for constructive dialogue between teacher and student and student and student. "Nor yet can dialogue exist without hope. Hope is rooted in men's incompletion, from which they move out in constant search – a search which can be carried out only in communion with others."[60] His understanding of the human condition, the knowledge that we are all incomplete in some way, infuses strength into our humility – even as he acknowledges that through communion with others, we can strive to move closer to completion. We gain strength through our communion. An optimal classroom environment is based on the coming together of all members of that community. This coming together, based upon the humility that comes with not-knowing, is energized, or fueled, by hope.

> As long as I fight, I am moved by hope; and if I fight with hope, then I can wait.

"Hopelessness," he writes, "is a form of silence, of denying the world and fleeing from it. Hope…does not consist in crossing one's arms and waiting. As long as I fight, I am moved by hope; and if I fight with hope, then I can wait."[61] We all know what it feels like to be lost in a classroom. The concept is supremely challenging, and it feels like you are the only person experiencing this sense of defeat. As a result, you cross your arms, sit back, and retreat from the discussion. You focus on not getting called out as you flee from the classroom environment. You experience this sense of hopelessness, waiting for the experience to end. There is no fight in you. You have given up. An excellent teacher will work to reignite that hope. She will notice that you are having an off moment or a bad day. She will use her own hope to fuel her compassionate response to your withdrawal, and she will utilize heartfelt efforts to return you to the class, knowing that you will not move ahead until that is achieved.

Students respond to teachers who present them in a hopeful light. They will work for them because they innately wish to perform for a teacher who has hope (belief) in them. This hope is communicated through individual connection and is present in many decisions a teacher makes. Ann Diederich, the language teacher from Polytechnic School in Pasadena, California,

---

60 Freire, Paulo (1968), *Pedagogy of the Oppressed* (New York: Penguin Education), p.72
61 Ibid.

recalls, "I don't allow my students to give up because by doing so I would be communicating that I don't believe in their potential. So I don't reduce my expectations in order to make my class easier for an individual. Doing so would contradict my sense of hope toward every student." The power of Ann's hope is clear here. She refuses to reduce expectations. As a result, she doesn't feed into their self-defeating mindset.

Yet hope is not regenerative in hostile environments. Hope takes time and effort to cultivate. It requires strength and demands belief in our students' better angels.

One of the more uncomfortable scenarios witnessed through classroom observations is the teacher who allows himself to get walked over because his hope has become a delusional fog. This happens to the teacher who hasn't yet generated his students' respect. He might be in the profession to be liked and affirmed. He might lack confidence in his subject mastery, and therefore choose to prioritize relationships over subject mastery. He might be the most heartfelt, empathetic, kind person, but if students don't know where that teacher is going in class, that teacher will get railroaded.

> Hope takes time and effort to cultivate. It requires strength and demands belief in our students' better angels.

History teacher Colleen Kyle from Lakeside School beautifully sums up the relationship between hope and perseverance by stating, "Hope is invested in the process, the faith that hard work and learning will get you your dreams. It sounds really corny, but it's the truth. It's like the poem on the foot of the Statue of Liberty – *The New Colossus*: 'Give me your tired, your poor, your masses, your need to breathe free.' It's sort of sentimental, but it's still true. That's what I think about hope in education."

Time to Factor in Faith

Teaching is a spiritual endeavor. We teach to student souls from our own. We do not simply upload information from our brains into our students' "open bucket skulls." Paulo Friere explains how learning is improved when a teacher relates to students in a shared dynamic instead of a teacher-centered interaction, with the teacher imparting information in a solely cognitive manner. "Narration (with the teacher as narrator) leads the students to memorize mechanically the narrated content. Worse yet, it turns them into 'containers,' into 'receptacles' to be 'filled' by the teacher. The more completely she fills the receptacles, the better a teacher she is. The more meekly the receptacles permit themselves to be filled the better students they are."

The best explanation I've read about the fact that teaching is not merely cognitive is written by Vanessa Rodriguez and Michelle Fitzpatrick in their book, *The Teaching Brain*. They state, "If teaching is simply a matter of training and following a basic input-output model of learning, that leaves us equipped to approximate teaching up to the developmental level of a chimp, dog, or bird."[62] Flattering description!

Finland-based Ressu Comprehensive School teacher Meghan Elizabeth observes, "I had this realization that I was trying to fill empty vessels, yet they are not empty and I don't need to fill them. It's a two-way street. They're teaching me. I'm teaching them."

As with learning, the act of teaching is also both cognitive and emotional. It is both prescriptive and steeped in possibility. It is an act of generosity. The optimal classroom environment assures that it is a two-way street: the teacher becomes the student becomes the teacher. Vanessa Rodriguez and Michelle Fitzpatrick state, "The concept of teaching as primarily a selfless act meant only to benefit the learner is fundamentally flawed by its unidirectional character. Devaluing or ignoring the teacher's context as part of the process does not acknowledge the act as a dynamic interaction. It's high time to ask ourselves if we are investing our time and money in education reforms that offer actual evidence of success."[63] The "dynamic interaction" between teacher and student is rooted in belief and faith – belief that the teacher believes in the student, and faith that the student will work earnestly and honestly.

> If teaching is simply a matter of training and following a basic input-output model of learning, that leaves us equipped to approximate teaching up to the developmental level of a chimp, dog, or bird.

This distinction between hope and faith fuels the inner life of expert teachers. We hope for snow days just like our students. And we have faith that Margot will grasp the concept or that Danny will get into the college that best suits him. Our faith bleeds into the less concrete, however, when we choose

---

62 Rodriguez, Vanessa and Fitzpatrick, Michelle (2014), *The Teaching Brain* (New York: The New Press), p.34
63 Ibid., p.30

what to focus on in our curriculum. Our faith guides us when we decide to shift gears mid-lesson because we sense that there is a more important gem to shine based on the classroom barometer. We have faith that when a student doesn't hand in his paper on time, he really did leave it in his sports bag back in New Hampshire. We have faith that when a student says, "I get it," she really means what she's saying and is not just placating the teacher. Our hope for a snow day comes from the ego – I *want* this. Our faith comes from somewhere deeper... our gut, our heart, and our soul.

> If the teacher can work from within by using her deep understanding of her student, she will be at her most effective.

Teachers who have deep reservoirs of hope for students are often teachers who take time to push, explore, and go the extra distance with them. The result is heightened levels of student engagement – because the student knows that the teacher believes in him. The trouble is that quantitative tests do not assess the impact of hope and engagement. Student engagement is not the same as student competency. This is why standardized testing cannot be fully accurate measurements for teacher efficacy.

In their article, "Meaningful Hope for Teachers in Times of High Anxiety and Low Morale," Drs. Carrie Nolan and Sarah M. Stitzlein acknowledge that the idea of hope in teaching conjures a stereotype of a relentlessly upbeat and cheerful teacher, unfazed and perhaps unaware of the world outside classroom walls. But they argue that a more accurate description of hope in teaching is what they call *pragmatist hope*.

A pragmatist hope is "located within and grows out of the muddy and complex circumstances of everyday life, rather than simply being applied regardless of circumstances."[64] Pragmatism takes into account the external variables that hinder the perfection of our society. Hope is found within this imperfect world. Pragmatist hope is found in the teacher who works with the individuals in the classroom, acknowledging that the end goal is not perfection, but inspiration and maximum student engagement. If the teacher can work from within by using her deep understanding of her student, she will be at her most effective.

In this way, efficacy is not assessed by summative data. It is not determined through student scores. Efficacy is only made genuine through the eyes of the

---

64 Nolan, Carrie and Stitzlein, Sarah M., 'Meaningful Hope for Teachers in Times of High Anxiety and Low Morale', *Democracy & Action* (Volume 19, Number 1) p.3

teacher herself. No one can place it on her – not an administrator, parent, or colleague. It is the honest self-assessment that understands both the goals of the lessons as well as the context (student abilities, personalities, time of day, day of week, week of year, etc.) in which these lessons are taught.

Hope springs from these "muddy and complex circumstances of everyday life," and it requires strength in order to burst through. Pragmatist hope is based on *melioration*, which is "the idea that at least there is a sufficient basis of goodness in life and its conditions so that by thought and earnest effort we may constantly make better things."[65] This resonated with me, and I suspect it also resonates with teachers reading this book.

This is because as teachers, we are hopeful – we have convictions based on the belief that each day can bring about new achievements, solutions, and discoveries that better our feelings about ourselves and the world in which we live. We believe in the benevolence inherent in this life, and that amidst the hardships and oppositions we can find grace, hope, and faith. I would argue that it is through being with younger people that our belief in the benevolence of the human soul is strengthened. Again, this model of hope is based on looking at the core and expanding outward from it. It is not a layering on of a rosy filter and soft, warm lighting. Hope is not a warm blanket – it is a tiny light in the core of our soul that can be given opportunities to shine forth when we apply "thought and earnest effort."

To envision the best takes strength and conviction, and sometimes a dash of self-delusion. As adults, we know we are flawed. We are imperfect. We certainly know that our students are imperfect as we strive to work together towards perfection, yet with the wisdom that achieving it is impossible. Therefore, it truly is only hope that we hold onto when we voyage with our students toward mastery, toward 'perfection.' It is hope that fuels our belief that today will contain several breakthroughs that will result from our hope-filled, relational teaching. We probably won't see these breakthroughs as they occur, as often they are within the mind and soul of the students; they are internal. However, we have hope that they will occur, and we have faith that they are occurring even when we don't have external proof.

When asked to reflect on the teachers who had the greatest impact on them, every person I interviewed acknowledged that it was the teachers who demonstrated faith that had the most long-lasting, positive influence. "The teachers who truly connected with me didn't have to," the artist Enrique Martínez Celaya states. "Yet even as a teenager, I knew these teachers were sacrificing time in order to connect with – rather – commit *to* me And this commitment came out from their faith in me."

65 Ibid.

Many teachers I interviewed for this book expressed feelings of deep gratitude for the faithful actions their teachers took to keep them engaged in school. There were teachers who helped inspire a love of books, numbers, science, or art. Most of all, I heard stories of teachers who gave their time to help with non-academic challenges. As Enrique says about the teachers who impacted him most, "Their care was unconditional and their rewards were the satisfaction of helping someone else." That is knowing the student. That is demonstrating faith in the student. That is real – and relational – teaching.

> I knew these teachers were sacrificing time in order to connect with – rather – commit to me And this commitment came out from their faith in me.

Time to Confirm Their Capabilities

Another means of hope is seeing students as capable and trusting in them by taking hope from students' potential. One means of doing so, as this can be challenging at times, is through what Nel Noddings puts forth as *confirmation*. Confirmation means looking for the best reason to explain a student's action. Homework not done? Rather than guessing the student was goofing off, confirmation means trying to imagine the best realistic reason. In doing so, "We confirm him; that is, we reveal to him an attainable image of himself that is lovelier than that manifested in his present acts. This does not mean ignoring the wrong, but attempting to correct it with a spirit of care and confirmation. This helps not only the student but the teacher as well, for when a student doesn't live up to expectations, a teacher can place this disappointment within a context of confirmation, understanding that there is more to the student than present manifestation."[66]

As I mentioned earlier, manifesting such hopes requires both strength and a dash of self-delusion. Both are required to present the student with a clear sense of their optimal self – the person they know deep inside they want to be, and the person their teacher communicates is completely possible to become.

In an article for PDK International's *Kappan* magazine, Kathleen Cushman, the author of *What Kids Can Do*, shared her "equation on motivation": Value x

---

66 Nolan, Carrie and, Sarah M., 'Meaningful Hope for Teachers in Times of High Anxiety and Low Morale', *Democracy & Action* (Volume 19, Number 1) p.8.

Expectancy = Motivation.[67] After interviewing hundreds of adolescents about the conditions that increase school motivation, she found eight commonalities. The Fifth Condition is that, "We have a Coach."

Cushman writes, "Students said they felt most motivated by teachers who acted like coaches in the classroom. Demonstrating new skills, providing support and encouragement, and helping them learn from their mistakes."

Indeed, 12-year-old Henry affirmed this Fifth Condition without knowing it – particularly the "providing support and encouragement" part of it. For that is the part that requires hope. And hope is what Henry was articulating when he described his ideal teacher traits. Coaches hold a high bar of potential, defined by clear description, and with a solid and unwavering level of critique that is both positive and negative. The implicit message of hope in coaching is, "You can be great. And I'm not going to shield you from identified obstacles that prevent you from being great."

> Manifesting such hopes requires both strength and a dash of self-delusion.

The efficacy of strictness is spotlighted in a study reported in *The Wall Street Journal* by Joanne Lipman. In it, she cites a study that focused on Los Angeles-based teachers whose students did exceptionally well. The researchers found that these teachers combined strictness with high expectations. Their core belief was, "Every student in my room is underperforming based on their potential, and it's my job to do something about it – and I can do something about it."

They interviewed a 4th grader, who described it as, "When I was in first grade and second grade and third grade, when I cried my teacher coddled me. When I go to Mrs. T's (the strict fourth grade teacher) room, she told me to suck it up and get to work. I think she's right. I need to work harder."[68] Of course, this approach only works when the teacher is able to discern the student's potential within the context of the day the student is having (i.e., is she feeling sick? Is she exceptionally tired? Is she showing laziness? Is she careless? Is she operating under false pretenses?). Moreover, this approach optimally works when the teacher has established a relational connection with the student based on trust and connection and steeped in hope.

---

67 Easton, Lois Brown (2014), *"Student Learning: Engagement and Motivation"* (Professional Development Discussion Guide) PDK International and Kappan Magazine (May, 2014) p.6

68 https://www.wsj.com/articles/why-tough-teachers-get-good-results-1380323772

Time to Reach Beyond the Comfort Zone

In his book, *The Talent Code*, Daniel Coyle argues that, "The trick [to mastery] is to choose a goal just beyond our present abilities; to target the struggle. Thrashing blindly doesn't help. Reaching does."[69] An effective coach or teacher runs an organized lesson that follows a pattern that is comforting in its clarity. The teacher knows how far his students can reach and, like a coach, pushes the student to master the "next level up."

The idea of teaching students to reach just beyond their comfort zone as a demonstration of hope is an intriguing one as it breaks down the bifurcated perspective that strictness is either bad or good. In some cases, strictness is very good – and it helps when a student can sense that it is grounded in hope. Researchers have found that being exposed to challenges – including "a hardass kind of teacher" – builds resilience and confidence. Lipman believes that students pick up an underlying faith in their ability to do better. In this case, faith is the more accurate word – more precise than hope – because it is the belief that the student could do better in spite of there being nothing concrete defending this belief. Lipman, the *Wall Street Journal* reporter, states, "There is something to be said about a teacher who is demanding and tough not because he thinks students will never learn but because he is absolutely certain that they will."[70]

> There is something to be said about a teacher who is demanding and tough not because he thinks students will never learn but because he is absolutely certain that they will.

Hope plays a significant part in student motivation as well. A teacher conveys hope to a student: hope rooted in a pragmatic understanding of the student's challenges. A teacher can inspire a student to generate hope within himself by exposing him to examples of people who have achieved their goals. Coyle believes that there are three ingredients to developing talent: Ignition; Master Coaching; and Deep Practice. Ignition is the event or role model that provides powerful motivation to work hard and a belief that excellent performance is achievable.

A teacher plays a significant role in coaxing that sense of hope in a student so that it is not a forgotten spark but instead a breathing fire. Suzanne Buck,

---

69 Coyle, Daniel (2010) *The Talent Code* (London: Arrow Books), p.19
70 https://www.wsj.com/articles/why-tough-teachers-get-good-results-1380323772

Suzanne Buck

the Head of School and Rector at Chatham Hall School, gives a great example of how some students were ignited into lighting a fire from their sparks when she talks about a teacher who walked into her math classroom to find her students deeply upset.

"They had just watched a YouTube video about animal extinction. Some were crying, and they were all talking about concerns about endangered species. This teacher knew that she had to get them into content mode. But instead of pushing through by putting curriculum first, she chose to utilize the example of extinction, talk about it in a hopeful way – about activism, and using activism as a lens where they can make a genuine difference." This small yet clear example of being flexible, meeting students "where they are", and applying content to real life experience in that moment hinges on growing hope. It is not "turn that frown upside-down;" rather, it is based in reality and charging the students as genuine agents of change. This example of relational teaching is empowering and hope-based, indeed.

Suzanne concludes, "The teacher was able to get those students back on task in terms of looking at activism and the positive results that spring forward from activism well-executed. That's an example of how relational teaching is using hope while teaching to the spirit."

Author Daniel Pink (*Drive, A Whole New Mind*) states that, "As teachers, as entire organizations, our instinct is toward greater control. We think control is going to make something better. But people have only two reactions to control: They comply or they defy. We don't want defiant kids, but we also don't want compliant kids. We want kids who are engaged. If you truly want to engage kids, you have to pull back on control and create the conditions in which they can tap into their own inner motivations."[71]

It is easy yet not entirely stimulating to teach to a class of compliant students. When teachers daydream about their ideal classroom, more often than not they envision a class of engaged learners, poring over the materials at hand and peacefully finding themselves in the flow of sustained inquiry. We don't envision compliance, which connotes an image of students working on their own, practicing perfect handwriting and dutifully coloring within the lines without disruption (or spirit). Compliance begets conformity. We see the "Stepford Wives" version of living and it's not an attractive look on children!

> Pulling back requires hope on behalf of the teacher toward students – a hope based on the idealized vision of who these students can be when given the agency to operate freely in the classroom.

What Pink is describing here is the teacher's role in growing student engagement. It seems counterintuitive, yet Pink is encouraging (and I am endorsing) the method of "pulling back" in order for students to push themselves forward. Students need teachers to trust them by giving them room to make their own successes and learn from their own mistakes. The action of pulling back derives from a deep and constant well of hope. Pulling back requires hope on behalf of the teacher toward students – a hope based on the idealized vision of who these students can be when given the agency to operate freely in the classroom. The teacher whom Suzanne referenced in the aforementioned example demonstrated what happens when relational expert teachers are permitted to channel and cultivate hope in – and with – their students.

The essence of hope in the classroom also relates to the feedback given to teachers. As an example, World Language teacher Ann Diederich shares an honest story about a surprising bit of criticism she received years ago. It initially stung, but upon reflection, it turned into one of the greatest feedback gifts she'd ever received.

---

71 http://www.ascd.org/publications/educational-leadership/sept14/vol72/num01/Motivated-to-Learn@-A-Conversation-with-Daniel-Pink.aspx

"One time, a few years ago, the curricular consultant for diversity and social justice visited my class and completely tore it apart. 'There is not enough *hope* in your lesson,' she told me. She wanted me to teach not only about the darkness of slavery, but also examples of positive change that ensued. She wanted me to focus on historic efforts to rectify, acknowledge, and reverse this ugly trend." Ann clarified that the curricular consultant was in no way asking her to go soft on the brutal facts. Instead, she wanted Ann to search for ways to be factual yet aspirational. The message was that if you're going to teach curricula containing facts that challenge the moral compass, it is helpful to balance it with examples of hope that can inspire impressionable and idealistic students to make future positive change. Following this feedback, Ann included stories about empowered freed slaves, the Peruvian government apologizing for slavery, and the Australian government acknowledging appropriating aboriginal land.

"A year later, the curricular consultant said, 'I was worried...I was really hard on you.' Yet it was the best professional experience I could have had at the time. She gave *me* hope in telling me to really move away from the content and deliberately build up a sense of hope for the better in my students. And I found that she was right. It really was what I needed to do."

By using her own authenticity, the curricular consultant built trust. As a result, Ann acknowledges, "I've been applying her feedback to my other classes as well ever since." The thrust of her advice to Ann was to always give students hope for the future. Situations can be improved or eradicated – even horrific and defenseless institutional policies encouraging slavery. By cultivating a sense of hope that taps into the idealism of adolescents, a relational teacher plants the seeds toward positive change in both the individual and society.

Time to Set the Pathway

Roxbury Latin School English teacher Rob Crawford sees hope in every student, and he speaks about it as only the son of a Boston minister can. "The student has to have hope of doing well in the class. He actually has to see a pathway to getting a positive grade so that he can feel proud. I think especially in English, a lot of kids just think, 'I have no chance of getting an A in this class. I guess I'm just striding for the B or B–.' I believe there has to be a pathway. A kid has to *believe* he can get an A– or an A in the class if he has the will and the work ethic. I think that's a very important kind of hope." The hope Rob describes is based on an unconditional belief in the positive potential in everyone. It acknowledges that any student can succeed, given the right teacher and classroom environment. The definition of success, however, differs based on the student.

I've always viewed part of the art of teaching as pulling from the top while pushing from the bottom. This idea is that every student has his or her own definition of success, and what might come easily to one student might be a real challenge to another. And that is alright. The teacher recognizes each one's strengths and challenges, and works with them with hope as a guiding principle.

Rob continues, "Teaching is all about learning. It's about setting the stage for learning and it is based on hope. I want my students to have hope that comes with the realization that your effort is related to your grade, even if you don't get the scores you need. It is sort of like if a kid is practicing extremely hard for sports. Practicing, working hard, he loses every game and he starts to wonder, 'What's the point of going to practice and working hard every day if I lose every game?' I sometimes give a student a win. I would be like, 'Because of your hard work you actually just get a win. I'm just going to give you a win.' That student will think he earned the B– when I objectively know the paper is a C. He believes he earned it. And as a result, he is more confident, participating more actively in class and demonstrating deeper engagement."

> I want my students to have hope that comes with the realization that your effort is related to your grade, even if you don't get the scores you need.

As a teacher, I did the same thing on rare occasions, in the belief that there are many students who could use a boost. Not strictly a grade boost, but rather the confidence boost that results from the grade. It's similar to the thrust one feels during a plane's climb to cruising altitude. During the climb, the plane sporadically glides for a few moments before thrusting forward with the nose pointed upwards again. During the plateau, there is a sinking feeling inside the cabin. After the thrust is applied, however, there is a definite forward (and upward) momentum. That's how it is with learning. Sometimes, a student plateaus. As he loses momentum, he sinks a bit. The benevolent grade, the "see me after class," the opportunity for a rewrite…all of these actions are boosters that cause renewed forward (and upward) momentum.

These boosters are all predicated on the hopeful idea that a student will thrust himself forward and regain his engagement through newly acquired confidence. Some might view this as unethical, as it promotes grades as subjective, doled out at the whim of the teacher. However, I would argue that teaching is about learning, and if a teacher clearly believes that a grade is a motivating tool (which I do), then an infrequent altering of a grade could in the long term serve as the thrust a student needs to return to a pathway toward success.

Rob observes, "It's about helping students realize that who they are as a person is way more important than what grade they get in any class." If who they are is defined as capable, intelligent, and possessing potential, then the grade is merely a tool toward a higher or lower self-concept. A hopeful teacher understands outside circumstances impact student performance, and he will view the grade as fair not fixed.

When I asked Rob about how he derives hope from teaching that motley age known as middle and high school students, he answered, "Sometimes tangents are where the real learning takes place. I take advantage of natural breaks in the lesson just to share wisdom with them. This is where I just share my deepest values. I'll say, 'I have to tell you something. Life is not like 9th grade, okay? I mean, you're all going to be successful in something.' You just tell them, 'Once you get to college you're all going to fall into your own little majors. When you get your job you're all going to find your expertise. You're all going to be amazing at it. Here you're all evaluated basically on how good a student you are. That's a special skill you're all learning. But that begins and ends here at school.'"

Laguna Blanca Middle School Director and world history teacher Steve Chan corroborates when he says, "I tell students that it will get better. I've been really lucky to see kids that I've known when they were 12 years old grow up into really good adults. And to know that the tough times that they'll face at this age will help to shape their personalities, and to make them into whole individuals. But that for most of them, they're going to turn out a-okay. And it's nice to see it on the other end when they become adults and they come back and they share. I love that."

The message that teachers communicate to students about the broadness of the world that lies ahead versus the narrowness of their current school existence relates to how students view success. If the focus is on the outcomes (i.e., grades), then high-achieving students are motivated to fixate on their

> Sometimes tangents are where the real learning takes place. I take advantage of natural breaks in the lesson just to share wisdom with them. This is where I just share my deepest values.

GPAs and class rank (paying attention to how they compare to their classmates). Too much focus on grades can lead students to trip on their own drive. They might view the classroom as a competitive environment rather than a collaborative one. Consequently, they may block out the wisdom of their peers as "not on the test." In this cutthroat world of college-based markers of K–12 success, such a perspective is understandable. An expert, relational teacher will notice this and work with the student to reflect on how the narrow, goal-fixated view can serve to stymie the joy of learning and make school feel like something to be "done" instead of appreciated.

> It's nice to see it on the other end when they become adults and they come back and they share. I love that.

Steve mentions that former students return to his classroom as adults and share stories about their adult lives. He "love(s) that," implying that there is a sense of fulfillment within a teacher that comes with recognizing his role along the way. Rob gives his students advanced notice about their adult lives. He tells them they will wind up in a world where evaluation and performance are assessed differently. The focus will not be on report cards, GPAs, SAT scores, and the like.

Expert relational teachers like Rob and Steve communicate hope to their students. Hope that they will use what they've learned to build a strong character and find success. Hope that they will return one day with colorful stories to share with the expert teachers who created optimal classroom environments based on understanding, respect, and empathy.

Recapping the Relational: Helplessly Hope

Paulo Freire asserts that hope is found "only in communion with others." The classroom provides that communion – that community – in which hope can flourish. Think about it – there are hundreds of individuals in most schools. These are hundreds of people to look toward for hope. There should be no shortage of hope in schools because optimal learning environments are generative. Expert teachers recognize that teaching is a spiritual endeavor and hope is a central component of the spirit. As Colleen Kyle referenced earlier, a teacher "treads lightly" on students' dreams. Dreams are hope-filled. A teacher is hope-full. When a teacher's hope is depleted, as in the case of Peggy toward Trevor, the walls close in and darkness falls into hopelessness.

Rob Crawford illustrates that when a teacher assigns a re-do, he is infusing the assignment with hope. This hope is revealed in the generous offering to raise the grade, and the implicit message is that the learning is more important than the "one-and-done" approach to graded assignments. Hope is exhibited by the belief that the student will not only *do* better but *learn* better when given the chance to re-do. There is hope that the student did not hit the expected mark for legitimate reasons that tend to happen at times in the chaotically busy life of today's adolescent. There is hope that the teacher communicates that who his student is (and is becoming) matters more than what the student produces at any given time. As with most examples of relational teaching, the student feels it, even if he cannot define it. This is a reminder that teaching is an art and a spiritual endeavor. We teach through words and actions and the student responds through feeling.

As is made clear from the beginning of this book, a teacher's job is to teach her students how to learn well and how to grow optimally. Yet they also represent the future through word and action. Students look for hope from their adult teachers who not only present themselves as content experts but also as life experts. This is not the same as being perfect in either content or life. Yet it is about being hopeful about both. This content is important to learn and I have hope that you will realize its importance through my teaching. Life is imperfect yet I hope you see me as someone exhibiting an ease with this fact. An expert teacher is a beacon of hope who can use that element in order to challenge and raise the bar in a way that encourages hard work. School is hard. Childhood and adolescence does not comprise a linear path of consistent sunny days. Yet if a classroom ethos is based on hope, students receive the message that all of this effort will help facilitate their brighter lives ahead.

Conclusion

"You teachers are always thinking, 'good class, bad class, good class, bad class, very good class'...but we just leave thinking, 'class, class, class, class, class.'"

Student, Philips Academy, Andover

"All my friends are here. I'm on the hockey team, I'm on the basketball team. I got to maintain a boat now. I work on George's boat two days a week, I got two girlfriends and I'm in a band."

Patrick (age 16), *Manchester by the Sea* (2016, Dir. Kenneth Lonergan)[72]

The quotes above communicate two facts. The first is that while students absolutely observe their teachers with acuity, they do not judge their instructional delivery with anything like the close scrutiny that teachers do of themselves. We are our own harshest critics. Part of this might come from the sense that our class is at the center of the students' world. This may appear to some as arrogant, but I view this myopia as an example of a teacher's pride in his classroom work. Another reason might be because teachers are so infrequently evaluated, we are generally left to ourselves to judge our classroom performance. We tend to put a great deal of importance on student

---

72 http://www.npr.org/2016/11/18/502560498/bleak-mournful-manchester-by-the-sea-packs-an-emotional-punch

reactions, leaving room for misinterpretation. Like Freud's "sometimes a cigar is just a cigar" comment, sometimes a tuned out student is just a tuned out student – not someone aggressively taking up arms against the teacher.

The other quote is spoken at the midpoint of the movie, when the nephew is taken in by his uncle, who has overlooked the dimensions of the life this 16-year-old leads. Teachers tend to do the same thing when giving assignments and setting expectations. It is easy to presume that students will put in the time for your class. Yet it is also easy to assume that your class holds more importance in the student's waking hours than it does. The world of a student today is arguably much like the world their parents grew up in. There are myriad electives, social events, and extracurricular activities keeping them busy outside of academics. They are busy, and they are under great pressure. Teachers need time to understand the time pressures their students are under – not so they can be more lenient and 'easy.' Rather, so that they can more seamlessly integrate their expectations into the reality of their students' worlds.

And we need to ease up.

Teaching is not a profession rooted in perfection. Teaching is more in line with a noble calling. In fact, of the nearly 100 teachers I interviewed, not one spoke about being perfect on the job. Many shared stories of imperfect experiences in the classroom, and how these situations enabled them to grow as both professionals and individuals. Like the builders of the Tower of Babel, we can strive for perfection and maintain the goal of being as God-like as possible. Yet we should not confuse striving for perfection as implying that perfection is achievable. This humble admission might be challenging to conceptualize if one is not a teacher.

In many careers, workers are assessed and evaluated through clear analytical measurements. We have strived to replicate such objective assessments for teachers, yet we have yet to do so effectively. Clinical and organizational psychologist and education consultant Rob Evans refers to this as the "Accountability Dilemma: the challenge of assessing and conveying the performance of the school and its teachers."[73]

In Finland, teachers are assessed against the national core curriculum and the individual school's strategic plan. Because there is no standardized testing in Finland, that measurement is not included. Despite the absence of those metrics, Finland's education system seems to be doing more than alright.

Relational teaching should be baked into teacher evaluation systems. A system that evaluates shared trust, openness to exploration, allowance for authenticity, connection, hope, and time for reflection in teaching is key

73 https://www.nais.org/magazine/independent-school/fall-2013/be-all-you-can-be/

toward growing teacher efficacy. Feedback from colleagues, parents, students, and administrators would be taken into account, with the most significant feedback coming from the teacher herself. Self-reflection is a meaningful core of teacher evaluation because the practice of it recognizes the fact that only the teacher spends the hours, days, and months in the classroom. The teacher's voice should be integral in the evaluation process.

Vanessa Rodriguez and Michelle Fitzpatrick equate the use of student test scores as sole tools for evaluation to an example in the medical field. "Utilizing student test scores to measure teaching is like using only a thermometer to determine whether you have the flu. A thermometer may tell you something about your condition, but it isn't designed to identify viruses, assess congestion, or evaluate levels of lethargy. We turn to other measures and the expertise of doctors for that, because that's what it takes to get a complete and accurate picture."[74]

> Utilizing student test scores to measure teaching is like using only a thermometer to determine whether you have the flu. A thermometer may tell you something about your condition, but it isn't designed to identify viruses, assess congestion, or evaluate levels of lethargy.

Each teacher interviewed for this book welcomed feedback and the accountability measures they represent. They also spoke of the importance of evaluation systems that include social-emotional teaching (SET) and social-emotional learning (SEL). In order to measure for each, an assessment needs to include room for the observation of the qualitative. This takes time, yet it is the only way for an evaluation to be effective. For me, being evaluated (regardless of its actual efficacy) was an experience that validated what I did in the silo-like classroom. I relished shutting the door and teaching in the sanctity of my own classroom. Yet I also appreciated the infrequent times I was able to open my door to someone else and share what was going on inside.

During my time spent travelling around the U.S. and Europe talking with expert teachers and students from public, private, charter, and community schools about relational teaching, I learned an immeasurable amount.

74 Rodriguez, Vanessa (2014), *The Teaching Brain* (New York: The New Press), p.22

Within the interviews completed, some through-lines became apparent. Most importantly the idea that learning is both cognitive and emotional. Relational teaching responds to this.

The courage to teach is heart-work and hard work. It is intellectual, emotional, and spiritual. I'd also add physical, as numerous teachers (and my own long memory of being a teacher) mention their sore feet, tried and tested bladders, strained eyes, and rigid metacarpals as evidence of a hard job. Add to this the intellectual (keeping up with the content), the emotional (gauging the IQ, EQ, and individual challenges and strengths of each student), and the spiritual (the hope, faith and love for each student and oneself), and the job becomes more than just hard work. It becomes noble, even transcendent, and impossible to view as capable of perfection.

Before writing this book, I wondered whether these interviews would convey the exhaustion of teaching. Some did. But what I also received on the other side of the fulcrum was a hundred times more powerful and insistent. "I didn't choose teaching; teaching chose me." "Teaching is a vocation and a calling – definitely not just a job." "Teaching has made my life rich in value and experience, if not money." "Because I have taught for so long, I know that my legacy will live on far after my earthly years." Tom Fennell, the language and history teacher from Sierra Canyon School in Chatsworth, sent me an email with the following request:

"Could you please include this tribute about my teacher, Sister Mary Mercedes Graber, who passed away in 1997. Sister Mary taught me Latin at Catholic Central High School in Troy, NY. She taught me Cicero in my junior year and Virgil in my senior year. All these years later, her passion and love of Latin is alive and well in my head. I find myself teaching things she taught me now over 50 years ago. Can you imagine? I often teach the kids using the exact formulae I learned from her so long ago. I hear her passionately reading and quoting her favorite lines from *The Aeneid*. Concerning my high school years, she is the greatest memory I have, the greatest inspiration."

Imbedded in Tom's tribute are words connoting the ethereal, the mystical, and the spiritual. Sister Mary was, for Tom, someone who continues to live "alive and well in my head." She is someone who, through her deeply effective teaching style, continues "reading and quoting her favorite lines." Her voice remains in Tom's head 50 years after her time spent with him. "Can you imagine?" he exclaims in disbelief, yet also with pride. I sense that Tom's pride also stems from the knowledge that he, too, has imbedded himself in the long-term memory banks of hundreds if not thousands of students who entered and exited his optimal classroom environment over the years.

Tom's tribute to Sister Mary defines the relational elements of her teaching.

She read to her students. She authentically shared her favorite lines from *The Aeneid*. She inspired him with her passion for Latin and her love for her students. Tom emulates Sister Mary in his teaching style. In that way, not only does she live in his memory, but her spirit is passed on to his students.

The power of an expert, relational teacher lasts for generations. Realizing this makes the profession of teaching something of a path toward immortality. If Socrates, Plato, and Aristotle remain "alive" in classrooms today for both their content and the stories of their lives from millennia ago, then so too can teachers today.

We are at the dawn of a new era in education. We are already witnessing the very first stages of putting neuroscience and psychology into action in the classroom. The connection between learning and emotions has opened up new channels of dialogue regarding how best to teach to individual students. Teachers are starting to focus on the social emotional side of learning using new technology-supported tools. Positive psychology has opened up new avenues of relational teaching that centers on broadening the mindset for learning through the creation of positive classroom environments. Technology is identifying new ways of transmitting information and relaying deeper feedback to teachers based on student responses.

Many schools are incorporating Social-Emotional Learning (SEL) programs into their daily schedules to overwhelmingly positive success. Teachers are using technology to connect with other teachers around the world. The material now accessible for teachers to mine is far richer than when I began teaching 25 years ago. With this being the case, the time is right to focus on the qualitative – the relational – side of teaching. We have the content at our fingertips. When focusing on pedagogy – the delivery of the content through teaching – we should include relational teaching.

> The power of an expert, relational teacher lasts for generations. Realizing this makes the profession of teaching something of a path toward immortality.

Epilogue

Ithaka gave you the marvelous journey.
Without her you would not have set out.
She has nothing left to give you now.

And if you find her poor, Ithaka won't have fooled you.
Wise as you will have become, so full of experience,
you will have understood by then what these Ithakas mean.

C. P. Cavafy, "Ithaka"

Tho' much is taken, much abides; and tho'
We are not now that strength which in old days
Moved earth and heaven, that which we are, we are;
One equal temper of heroic hearts,
Made weak by time and fate, but strong in will
To strive, to seek, to find, and not to yield.

Alfred, Lord Tennyson, "Ulysses"

The relationship between teacher and student is based on knowing the other. And time is required to cultivate this relationship and ground it in love. Several teachers I spoke with mentioned love as the preeminent emotion when describing why they teach. This love is based on belief and faith. It presents itself through hope and is built by trust-based connection. Teacher and students share the adventure that comes through exploration, and the time spent on reflection not only solidifies knowledge but also permits a pause. This love is achieved when the teacher and the students are invited to be honest versions of their best selves – acknowledging their assets and their detriments, striving toward individual goals (academic and personal), and allowing for failure along the way.

My father was a classroom teacher and remains a sailor today. He taught me everything I know about the ocean. I take from his lessons an outlook on teaching that is governed by the principles of sailing. As I conclude this book, I reflect on my father's lessons imparted to me and the ways they've been applied toward my understanding of the organic nature of the classroom.

Several teachers I spoke with mentioned love as the preeminent emotion when describing why they teach.

I've used the sailing analogy on numerous occasions when speaking with parents. Sailing is relational. It is about interacting with the elements of nature, not against nature. In order to most effectively sail, one must acknowledge the personality of the conditions. What direction is the wind coming from? What direction are the waves coming from? How strong is the wind? How consistent? How predictable? Are there spontaneous outbursts from the wind? Do the waves obstruct my boat getting to where it needs to be or do they glide me toward that object?

A sailor's deep connection to the sea is based on head and heart. There is time on the water and also time spent away from the water – a restoration that takes place with objective distance. The ocean contains secrets and surprises underneath its surface, as do our students, who at times amaze us by their depth of thinking and understanding. The moon impacts the ocean tides; external conditions, situations, and events impact our students. Expert teachers know how to read the barometer of the class and tailor their teaching to it, as opposed to battling it in a vain attempt to change what's real. To expert teachers, a student is not an adversary, but rather a mysterious source of wisdom and strength. The expert teacher knows that there is no cheating in teaching. There are only sailboats. There are no motorboats to push ahead at a speed beyond the pace of learning.

We give preeminence to the relational when we teach students. Technology is integrated mindfully with the goal of enhanced learning for greater depth. The depth of student understanding is like the depth of the ocean. We sail along the surface while teaching, but we seek opportunities to go deep and plunge into the unknown with our students sometimes leading the way. Expert teachers understand that the essence of expert teaching involves surrender and vulnerability.

In this way, we lead our classrooms with an understanding that teaching is messy; the human condition is messy. We do not allow for egregious mistakes in character. Yet we do allow for the sudden wind gust, anticipated only by ripples on the water approaching our boat. We allow for a change in direction only if it makes the most sense based on the barometer of the class. We keep our eyes on the long horizon ahead, fixed on the marker buoy and unwavering toward its destination. We know that the route to our goal is broad and circuitous based on human elements.

Yet we, as teachers at the helm of a class, convey a certainty to our students working the lines and charting the course. This certainty, backed up by confidence that comes through organization and planning, gives our students a sense of security and stability. There is no electron-cloud of anxiety preventing the learning from being transferred. Instead, there is a low hum of excitement that comes with the shared experience of arriving at a destination together. This is true education. This is genuine learning that weaves time as its most essential element. This is the relational teaching that arises when we have time to teach and time to reach.